UNDERSTANDING AND USING

ENGLISH GRAMMAR

Third Edition

CHARTBOOK
A Reference Grammar

Betty Schrampfer Azar

Longman

Editorial director: *Allen Ascher*
Executive editor: *Louisa Hellegers*
Development editor: *Janet Johnston*
Director of design and production: *Rhea Banker*
Associate director of electronic publishing: *Aliza Greenblatt*
Managing editor: *Shelley Hartle*
Electronic production editors: *Rachel Baumann, Nicole Dawson*
Associate art director: *Carey Davies*
Manufacturing manager: *Patrice Fraccio*
Production manager: *Ray Keating*
Manufacturing buyer: *Edith Pullman*
Illustrator: *Don Martinetti*

© 2000 by Betty Schrampfer Azar

Published by Pearson Education
10 Bank Street, White Plains, N.Y. 10606

Printed in the United States of America
10 9 8 7

ISBN 0-13-958703-9

CONTENTS

Chapter 5 ADVERB CLAUSES OF TIME AND REVIEW OF VERB TENSES

Chapter 6 SUBJECT–VERB AGREEMENT

Chapter 7 NOUNS

Chapter 8 PRONOUNS

Chapter 9 MODALS, PART 1

Preface

This is a reference grammar for students of English as a second or foreign language. With a minimum of terminology and a broad table of contents, it seeks to make essential grammar understandable and easily accessible. The charts are concise presentations of information that second/foreign language learners want and need to know in order to use English clearly, accurately, and communicatively.

Intended as a useful tool for students and teachers alike, the *Chartbook* can be used alone as a desk reference or in conjunction with the *Workbook*. The practices in the *Workbook* are keyed to the charts in the *Chartbook*.

In the *Workbook*, the answers are given to all the practices. The *Chartbook/Workbook* combination allows learners to study independently. Upper-level students can work through much of the grammar on their own. They can investigate and correct their usage problems, as well as expand their usage repertoire, by doing selfstudy practices in the *Workbook*; they can find answers to most of their grammar questions in the charts in the *Chartbook*.

Writing classes (or other courses, tutorials, or rapid reviews in which grammar is not the main focus but needs attention) may find the *Chartbook/Workbook* combination especially useful.

Differences in structure usage between American and British English are noted throughout the text. The differences are few and relatively insignificant.

The *Teacher's Guide* for *Understanding and Using English Grammar* contains additional notes on many grammar points; each chart is discussed and amplified in some way.

Acknowledgments

The support I receive from the publishing professionals I work with is much appreciated. I wish specifically to thank Shelley Hartle for directing this project and, along with Janet Johnston, seeing every aspect of this project through from beginning to end. I admire their professionalism and value their cheerful friendship. They are two very special and wonderful people.

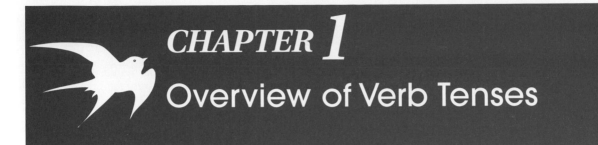

CHAPTER 1
Overview of Verb Tenses

The diagram shown below will be used in the tense descriptions:

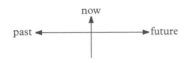

1-1 THE SIMPLE TENSES

TENSE	EXAMPLES	MEANING
SIMPLE PRESENT	(a) It *snows* in Alaska. (b) Tom *watches* television every day.	In general, the simple present expresses events or situations that exist *always, usually, habitually;* they exist now, have existed in the past, and probably will exist in the future.
SIMPLE PAST	(c) It *snowed* yesterday. (d) Tom *watched* television last night.	*At one particular time in the past,* this happened. It began and ended in the past.
SIMPLE FUTURE	(e) It *will snow* tomorrow. It *is going to snow* tomorrow. (f) Tom *will watch* television tonight. Tom *is going to watch* television tonight.	*At one particular time in the future,* this will happen.

1-2 THE PROGRESSIVE TENSES

Form: **be** + **-ing** (*present participle*)
Meaning: The progressive tenses* give the idea that an action is in progress during a particular time.
The tenses say that an action *begins before*, *is in progress during*, and *continues after* another time or action.

PRESENT PROGRESSIVE	(a) Tom *is sleeping* right now.	It is now 11:00. Tom went to sleep at 10:00 tonight, and he is still asleep. His sleep began in the past, *is in progress at the present time*, and probably will continue.
PAST PROGRESSIVE	(b) Tom *was sleeping* when I arrived.	Tom went to sleep at 10:00 last night. I arrived at 11:00. He was still asleep. His sleep began before and *was in progress at a particular time in the past*. It continued after I arrived.
FUTURE PROGRESSIVE	(c) Tom *will be sleeping* when we arrive.	Tom will go to sleep at 10:00 tomorrow night. We will arrive at 11:00. The action of sleeping will begin before we arrive, and it *will be in progress at a particular time in the future*. Probably his sleep will continue.

*The progressive tenses are also called the "continuous" tenses: present continuous, past continuous, and future continuous.

Tom *is washing* the dishes right now.

1-3 THE PERFECT TENSES

Form: **have** + *past participle*
Meaning: The perfect tenses all give the idea that one thing *happens before* another time or event.

PRESENT PERFECT eat / now (time?)	(a) Tom *has* already *eaten*.	Tom *finished* eating *sometime before now*. The exact time is not important.
PAST PERFECT eat / arrive	(b) Tom *had* already *eaten* when his friend arrived.	First Tom finished eating. Later his friend arrived. Tom's eating was completely *finished before another time in the past.*
FUTURE PERFECT eat / arrive	(c) Tom *will* already *have eaten* when his friend arrives.	First Tom will finish eating. Later his friend will arrive. Tom's eating will be completely *finished before another time in the future.*

1-4 THE PERFECT PROGRESSIVE TENSES

Form: **have** + **been** + **-ing** (*present participle*)
Meaning: The perfect progressive tenses give the idea that one event is *in progress immediately before, up to, until another time or event.* The tenses are used to express the *duration* of the first event.

PRESENT PERFECT PROGRESSIVE 2 hrs.	(a) Tom *has been studying* for two hours.	Event in progress: studying. When? *Before now, up to now.* How long? For two hours.
PAST PERFECT PROGRESSIVE 2 hrs.	(b) Tom *had been studying* for two hours before his friend came.	Event in progress: studying. When? *Before another event in the past.* How long? For two hours.
FUTURE PERFECT PROGRESSIVE 2 hrs.	(c) Tom *will have been studying* for two hours by the time his friend arrives.	Event in progress: studying. When? *Before another event in the future.* How long? For two hours.

1-5 SUMMARY CHART OF VERB TENSES

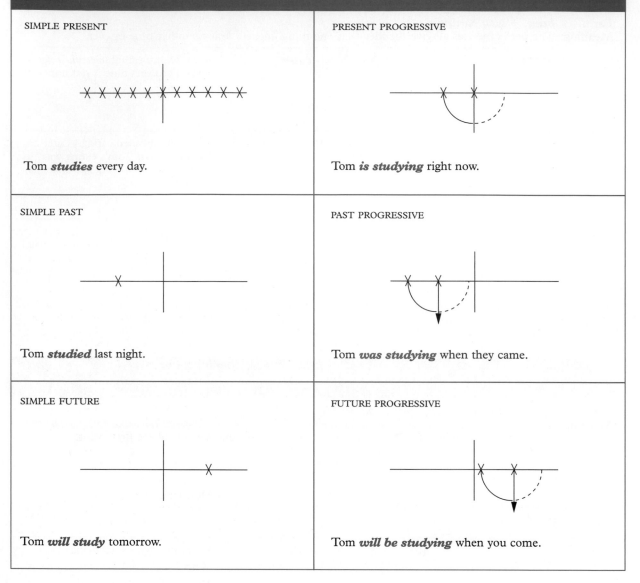

SIMPLE PRESENT

Tom **studies** every day.

PRESENT PROGRESSIVE

Tom **is studying** right now.

SIMPLE PAST

Tom **studied** last night.

PAST PROGRESSIVE

Tom **was studying** when they came.

SIMPLE FUTURE

Tom **will study** tomorrow.

FUTURE PROGRESSIVE

Tom **will be studying** when you come.

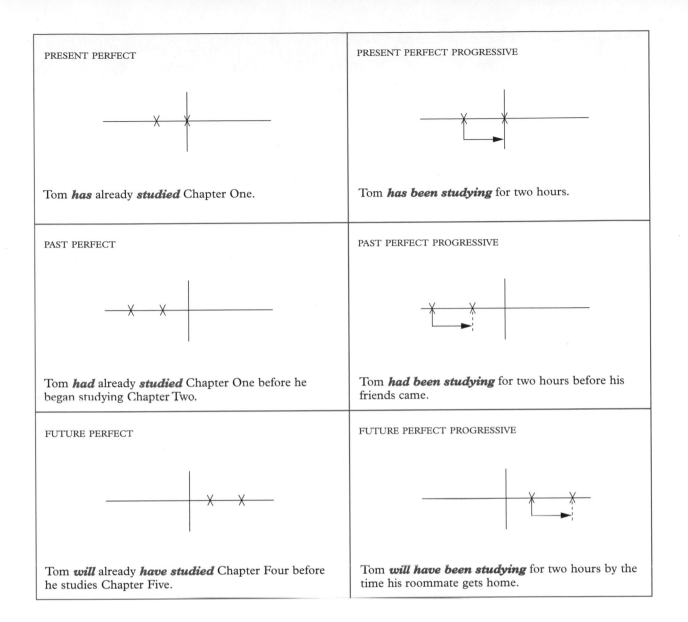

PRESENT PERFECT

Tom **has** already **studied** Chapter One.

PRESENT PERFECT PROGRESSIVE

Tom **has been studying** for two hours.

PAST PERFECT

Tom **had** already **studied** Chapter One before he began studying Chapter Two.

PAST PERFECT PROGRESSIVE

Tom **had been studying** for two hours before his friends came.

FUTURE PERFECT

Tom **will** already **have studied** Chapter Four before he studies Chapter Five.

FUTURE PERFECT PROGRESSIVE

Tom **will have been studying** for two hours by the time his roommate gets home.

1-6 SPELLING OF -ING AND -ED FORMS

(1)	VERBS THAT END IN A CONSONANT AND **-E**	(a) hope date injure	hoping dating injuring	hoped dated injured	**-ING** FORM: If the word ends in **-e**, drop the **-e** and add **-ing**.★ **-ED** FORM: If the word ends in a consonant and **-e**, just add **-d**.
(2)	VERBS THAT END IN A VOWEL AND A CONSONANT	ONE-SYLLABLE VERBS			
		(b) stop rob beg	stopping robbing begging	stopped robbed begged	*1 vowel → 2 consonants*★★
		(c) rain fool dream	raining fooling dreaming	rained fooled dreamed	*2 vowels → 1 consonant*
		TWO-SYLLABLE VERBS			
		(d) lísten óffer ópen	listening offering opening	listened offered opened	*1st syllable stressed → 1 consonant*
		(e) begín prefér contról	beginning preferring controlling	(began) preferred controlled	*2nd syllable stressed → 2 consonants*
(3)	VERBS THAT END IN TWO CONSONANTS	(f) start fold demand	starting folding demanding	started folded demanded	If the word ends in two consonants, just add the ending.
(4)	VERBS THAT END IN **-Y**	(g) enjoy pray buy	enjoying praying buying	enjoyed prayed (bought)	If **-y** is preceded by a vowel, keep the **-y**.
		(h) study try reply	studying trying replying	studied tried replied	If **-y** is preceded by a consonant: **-ING** FORM: keep the **-y**, add **-ing**. **-ED** FORM: change **-y** to **-i**, add **-ed**.
(5)	VERBS THAT END IN **-IE**	(i) die lie	dying lying	died lied	**-ING** FORM: Change **-ie** to **-y**, add **-ing**. **-ED** FORM: Add **-d**.

★Exception: If a verb ends in **-ee**, the final **-e** is not dropped: *seeing, agreeing, freeing.*

★★Exception: **-w** and **-x** are not doubled: *plow → plowed; fix → fixed.*

CHAPTER 2
Present and Past, Simple and Progressive

2-1 SIMPLE PRESENT

✗✗✗✗✗✗✗✗✗✗✗ (timeline)	(a) Water **consists** of hydrogen and oxygen. (b) The average person **breathes** 21,600 times a day. (c) The world **is** round.	The simple present says that something was true in the past, is true in the present, and will be true in the future. It expresses *general statements of fact and timeless truths.*
	(d) I **study** for two hours *every night*. (e) I **get** up at seven *every morning*. (f) He *always* **eats** a sandwich for lunch.	The simple present is used to express *habitual or everyday activities.*

2-2 PRESENT PROGRESSIVE

start — now — finish? in progress (timeline)	(g) John **is sleeping** right now. (h) I need an umbrella because it **is raining**. (i) The students **are sitting** at their desks right now.	The present progressive expresses an activity that is *in progress at the moment of speaking.* It is a temporary activity that began in the past, is continuing at present, and will probably end at some point in the future.
	(j) I **am taking** five courses this semester. (k) John **is trying** to improve his work habits. (l) Susan **is writing** another book this year.	Often the activity is of a general nature: something generally in progress this week, this month, this year. Note (l): The sentence means that writing a book is a general activity Susan is engaged in at present, but it does not mean that at the moment of speaking she is sitting at her desk with pen in hand.

(a) Yum! This food **tastes** good. I **like** it very much. (b) *INCORRECT:* This food *is tasting* good. I *am liking* it very much.	Some English verbs have *stative* meanings. They describe states: conditions or situations that exist. When verbs have stative meanings, they are usually not used in progressive tenses. In (a): **tastes** and **like** have stative meanings. Each describes a state that exists.

(c) The chef is in his kitchen.
He **is tasting** the sauce.
(d) It **tastes** too salty.
(e) He **doesn't like** it.

A verb such as **taste** has a *stative* meaning, but also a *progressive* meaning. In (c): **tasting** describes the action of the chef putting something in his mouth and actively testing its flavor (progressive). In (d): **tastes** describes the person's awareness of the quality of the food (stative).

A verb such as **like** has a stative meaning. It is rarely, if ever, used in progressive tenses.

In (e): It is incorrect to say *He isn't liking it.*

The chef is tasting the sauce. It tastes too salty. He doesn't like it.

COMMON VERBS THAT HAVE STATIVE MEANINGS

Note: Verbs with an asterisk (*) are like the verb **taste**: they can have both stative and progressive meanings and uses.

(1) MENTAL STATE	know realize understand recognize	believe feel suppose think*	imagine* doubt* remember* forget*	want* need desire mean*
(2) EMOTIONAL STATE	love like appreciate please prefer	hate dislike fear envy	mind care	astonish amaze surprise
(3) POSSESSION	possess	have*	own	belong
(4) SENSE PERCEPTIONS	taste* smell*	hear feel*	see*	
(5) OTHER EXISTING STATES	seem look* appear* sound resemble look like	cost* owe weigh* equal	be* exist matter	consist of contain include*

2-4 AM / IS / ARE BEING + ADJECTIVE

(a) Ann *is sick* today. Alex *is nervous* about the exam. Tom *is tall* and *handsome*.	*Be* + *an adjective* usually expresses a stative meaning, as in the examples in (a). (See Appendix Chart A-3, p. A2, for information about adjectives.)
(b) Jack doesn't feel well, but he refuses to see a doctor. He *is being foolish*. (c) Sue *is being* very *quiet* today. I wonder if anything is wrong.	Sometimes main verb *be* + *an adjective* is used in the progressive. It is used in the progressive when it describes temporary, in-progress *behavior*. In (b): Jack's foolishness is temporary and probably uncharacteristic of him.
(d) *INCORRECT:* Mr. Smith *is being* old. *CORRECT:* Mr. Smith *is old*.	In (d): Age does not describe a temporary behavior. *Be* + *old* cannot be used in the progressive. Examples of other adjectives that cannot be used with *am/is/are being:* angry, beautiful, handsome, happy, healthy, hungry, lucky, nervous, sick, tall, thirsty, young.

ADJECTIVES THAT CAN BE USED WITH *AM/IS/ARE BEING*

bad (ill-behaved)	good (well-behaved)	loud	responsible
careful	illogical	nice	rude
cruel	impolite	noisy	serious
fair	irresponsible	patient	silly
foolish	kind	pleasant	unfair
funny	lazy	polite	unkind
generous	logical	quiet	unpleasant

Martha is doing an experiment with dangerous chemicals. She *is being careful*.

2-5 REGULAR AND IRREGULAR VERBS

REGULAR VERBS: The simple past and past participle end in *-ed*.				English verbs have four principal parts:
SIMPLE FORM	SIMPLE PAST	PAST PARTICIPLE	PRESENT PARTICIPLE	(1) simple form
hope	*hoped*	*hoped*	*hoping*	(2) simple past
stop	*stopped*	*stopped*	*stopping*	(3) past participle
listen	*listened*	*listened*	*listening*	(4) present participle
study	*studied*	*studied*	*studying*	
start	*started*	*started*	*starting*	
IRREGULAR VERBS: The simple past and past participle do not end in *-ed*.				Some verbs have irregular past forms.
SIMPLE FORM	SIMPLE PAST	PAST PARTICIPLE	PRESENT PARTICIPLE	Most of the irregular verbs in English are given in the alphabetical list in Chart 2-7, p. 12.
break	**broke**	**broken**	*breaking*	
come	**came**	**come**	*coming*	
find	**found**	**found**	*finding*	
hit	**hit**	**hit**	*hitting*	
swim	**swam**	**swum**	*swimming*	

Alexei **played** the violin on stage last night.
He *has **played*** before audiences many times.
We **went** to hear him play last night.
We *have **gone*** to several of his concerts.

2-6 REGULAR VERBS: PRONUNCIATION OF -ED ENDINGS

Final **-ed** has three different pronunciations: /t/, /d/, and /əd/.	
(a) *looked → look*/t/ *clapped → clap*/t/ *missed → miss*/t/ *watched → watch*/t/ *finished → finish*/t/ *laughed → laugh*/t/	Final **-ed** is pronounced /t/ after voiceless sounds. Voiceless sounds are made by pushing air through your mouth; no sound comes from your throat. Examples of voiceless sounds: "k," "p," "s," "ch," "sh," "f."
(b) *smell → smell*/d/ *saved → save*/d/ *cleaned → clean*/d/ *robbed → rob*/d/ *played → play*/d/	Final **-ed** is pronounced /d/ after voiced sounds. Voiced sounds come from your throat. If you touch your neck when you make a voiced sound, you can feel your voice box vibrate. Examples of voiced sounds: "l," "v," "n," "b," and all vowel sounds.
(c) *decided → decide*/əd/ *needed → need*/əd/ *wanted → want*/əd/ *invited → invite*/əd/	Final **-ed** is pronounced /əd/ after "t" and "d" sounds. The sound /əd/ adds a whole syllable to a word. COMPARE: *looked* = one syllable → look/t/ *smelled* = one syllable → smell/d/ *needed* = two syllables → need/əd/ *wanted* = two syllables → want/əd/

She *mopped* the kitchen floor,
vacuumed the carpet, and
dusted the furniture.

Note: Verbs followed by a bullet (•) are defined at the end of the list.

SIMPLE FORM	SIMPLE PAST	PAST PARTICIPLE	SIMPLE FORM	SIMPLE PAST	PAST PARTICIPLE
arise	arose	arisen	forbid	forbade	forbidden
be	was,were	been	forecast•	forecast	forecast
bear	bore	borne/born	forget	forgot	forgotten
beat	beat	beaten/beat	forgive	forgave	forgiven
become	became	become	forsake•	forsook	forsaken
begin	began	begun	freeze	froze	frozen
bend	bent	bent	get	got	gotten/got*
bet•	bet	bet	give	gave	given
bid•	bid	bid	go	went	gone
bind•	bound	bound	grind•	ground	ground
bite	bit	bitten	grow	grew	grown
bleed	bled	bled	hang**	hung	hung
blow	blew	blown	have	had	had
break	broke	broken	hear	heard	heard
breed•	bred	bred	hide	hid	hidden
bring	brought	brought	hit	hit	hit
broadcast•	broadcast	broadcast	hold	held	held
build	built	built	hurt	hurt	hurt
burn	burned/burnt	burned/burnt	keep	kept	kept
burst•	burst	burst	kneel	kneeled/knelt	kneeled/knelt
buy	bought	bought	know	knew	known
cast•	cast	cast	lay	laid	laid
catch	caught	caught	lead	led	led
choose	chose	chosen	lean	leaned/leant	leaned/leant
cling•	clung	clung	leap	leaped/leapt	leaped/leapt
come	came	come	learn	learned/learnt	learned/learnt
cost	cost	cost	leave	left	left
creep•	crept	crept	lend	lent	lent
cut	cut	cut	let	let	let
deal•	dealt	dealt	lie	lay	lain
dig	dug	dug	light	lighted/lit	lighted/lit
do	did	done	lose	lost	lost
draw	drew	drawn	make	made	made
dream	dreamed/dreamt	dreamed/dreamt	mean	meant	meant
eat	ate	eaten	meet	met	met
fall	fell	fallen	mislay	mislaid	mislaid
feed	fed	fed	mistake	mistook	mistaken
feel	felt	felt	pay	paid	paid
fight	fought	fought	put	put	put
find	found	found	quit***	quit	quit
fit	fit/fitted	fit/fitted	read	read	read
flee•	fled	fled	rid	rid	rid
fling•	flung	flung	ride	rode	ridden
fly	flew	flown	ring	rang	rung

*In British English: *get–got–got*. In American English: *get–got–gotten/got*.

Hang* is a regular verb when it means to kill someone with a rope around his/her neck. COMPARE: *I **hung my clothes in the closet. They **hanged** the murderer by the neck until he was dead.*

***Also possible in British English: *quit–quitted–quitted*.

SIMPLE FORM	SIMPLE PAST	PAST PARTICIPLE	SIMPLE FORM	SIMPLE PAST	PAST PARTICIPLE
rise	rose	risen	spring•	sprang/sprung	sprung
run	ran	run	stand	stood	stood
say	said	said	steal	stole	stolen
see	saw	seen	stick	stuck	stuck
seek•	sought	sought	sting•	stung	stung
sell	sold	sold	stink•	stank/stunk	stunk
send	sent	sent	strike•	struck	struck/stricken
set	set	set	strive•	strove/strived	striven/strived
shake	shook	shaken	string	strung	strung
shed•	shed	shed	swear	swore	sworn
shine	shone/shined	shone/shined	sweep	swept	swept
shoot	shot	shot	swim	swam	swum
show	showed	shown/showed	swing•	swung	swung
shrink•	shrank/shrunk	shrunk	take	took	taken
shut	shut	shut	teach	taught	taught
sing	sang	sung	tear	tore	torn
sink•	sank	sunk	tell	told	told
sit	sat	sat	think	thought	thought
sleep	slept	slept	throw	threw	thrown
slide•	slid	slid	thrust•	thrust	thrust
slit•	slit	slit	understand	understood	understood
smell	smelled/smelt	smelled/smelt	undertake	undertook	undertaken
speak	spoke	spoken	upset	upset	upset
speed	sped/speeded	sped/speeded	wake	woke/waked	woken/waked
spell	spelled/spelt	spelled/spelt	wear	wore	worn
spend	spent	spent	weave•	wove	woven
spill	spilled/spilt	spilled/spilt	weep•	wept	wept
spin•	spun	spun	win	won	won
spit	spit/spat	spit/spat	wind•	wound	wound
split•	split	split	withdraw	withdrew	withdrawn
spoil	spoiled/spoilt	spoiled/spoilt	write	wrote	written
spread•	spread	spread			

•Definitions of some of the less frequently used irregular verbs:

bet . . . . . . wager; offer to pay money if one loses

bid . . . . . . make an offer of money, usually at a public sale

bind . . . . . fasten or secure

breed . . . . . bring animals together to produce young

broadcast . . send information by radio waves; announce

burst . . . . . explode; break suddenly

cast . . . . . . throw

cling . . . . . hold on tightly

creep . . . . . crawl close to the ground; move slowly and quietly

deal . . . . . . distribute playing cards to each person; give attention to (deal with)

flee . . . . . . escape; run away

fling . . . . . throw with force

forecast . . . predict a future occurrence

forsake . . . abandon or desert

grind . . . . crush, reduce to small pieces

seek . . . . . look for

shed . . . . . drop off or get rid of

shrink . . . . become smaller

sink . . . . . move downward, often under water

slide . . . . . glide smoothly; slip or skid

slit . . . . . . cut a narrow opening

spin . . . . . turn rapidly around a central point

split . . . . . divide into two or more parts

spread . . . push out in all directions (e.g., butter on bread, news)

spring . . jump or rise suddenly from a still position

sting . . . cause pain with a sharp object (e.g., pin) or bite (e.g., by an insect)

stink . . . have a bad or foul smell

strike . . hit something with force

strive . . try hard to achieve a goal

swing . . move back and forth

thrust . . push forcibly; shove

weave . . form by passing pieces of material over and under each other (as in making baskets, cloth)

weep . . . cry

wind . . . (sounds like *find*) turn around and around

2-8 TROUBLESOME VERBS: *RAISE / RISE, SET / SIT, LAY / LIE*

TRANSITIVE	INTRANSITIVE	
(a) *raise, raised, raised* Tom **raised** his hand.	(b) *rise, rose, risen* The sun **rises** in the east.	**Raise, set,** and **lay** are *transitive* verbs; they are followed by an object. **Rise, sit,** and **lie** are *intransitive;* i.e., they are NOT followed by an object.*
(c) *set, set, set* I **will set** the book on the desk.	(d) *sit, sat, sat* I **sit** in the front row.	In (a): **raised** is followed by the object **hand**. In (b): **rises** is not followed by an object.
(e) *lay, laid, laid* I **am laying** the book on the desk.	(f) *lie,** lay, lain* He **is lying** on his bed.	Note: **Lay** and **lie** are troublesome for native speakers too and are frequently misused.

*See Appendix Chart A-1, p. A1, for information about transitive and intransitive verbs.

Lie is a regular verb **(lie, lied)** when it means "not tell the truth": *He lied to me about his age.*

2-9 SIMPLE PAST

	(a) I **walked** to school yesterday. (b) John **lived** in Paris for ten years, but now he *lives* in Rome. (c) I **bought** a new car three days ago.	The simple past indicates that an activity or situation *began and ended at a particular time in the past.*
	(d) Rita **stood** under a tree *when it* **began** *to rain.* (e) *When Mrs. Chu heard a strange noise*, she **got** up to investigate. (f) *When I* **dropped** *my cup*, the coffee **spilled** on my lap.	If a sentence contains **when** and has the simple past in both clauses, the action in the *when* clause happens first. In (d): 1st: The rain began. 2nd: She stood under a tree.

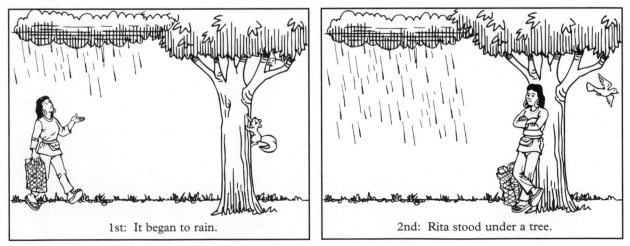

1st: It began to rain.　　　　2nd: Rita stood under a tree.

Rita **stood** under a tree when it **began** to rain.

2-10 PAST PROGRESSIVE

(g) I **was walking** down the street when it began to rain.

(h) While I **was walking** down the street, it began to rain.

(i) Rita **was standing** under a tree when it began to rain.

(j) At eight o'clock last night, I **was studying**.

(k) Last year at this time, I **was attending** school.

In (g): 1st: I was walking down the street.
2nd: It began to rain.
Both actions occurred at the same time, but *one action began earlier and was in progress when the other action occurred.*

In (j): My studying began before 8:00, was in progress at that time, and probably continued.

(l) While I **was studying** in one room of our apartment, my roommate **was having** a party in the other room.

Sometimes the past progressive is used in both parts of a sentence when two actions are in progress simultaneously.

1st: Rita stood under a tree.

2nd: It began to rain.

Rita **was standing** under a tree when it **began** to rain.

2-11 USING PROGRESSIVE VERBS WITH *ALWAYS* TO COMPLAIN

(a) Mary *always leaves* for school at 7:45.	In sentences referring to present time, usually the simple present is used with *always* to describe habitual or everyday activities, as in (a).
(b) Mary *is always leaving* her dirty socks on the floor for me to pick up! Who does she think I am? Her maid?	In special circumstances, a speaker may use the present progressive with *always* to complain, i.e., to express annoyance or anger, as in (b).*
(c) I *am always* / *forever* / *constantly picking* up Mary's dirty socks!	In addition to *always,* the words *forever* and *constantly* are also used with the present progressive to express annoyance.
(d) I didn't like having Sam for my roommate last year. He *was always leaving* his dirty clothes on the floor.	*Always, forever,* and *constantly* can also be used with the past progressive to express annoyance or anger.

*COMPARE:
  (1) *"Mary is always leaving her dirty socks on the floor"* expresses annoyance.
  (2) *"Mary always leaves her dirty socks on the floor"* is a statement of fact in which the speaker is not necessarily expressing an attitude of annoyance. Annoyance may, however, be shown by the speaker's tone of voice.

2-12 USING EXPRESSIONS OF PLACE WITH PROGRESSIVE VERBS

(a) —What is Kay doing?
   — She*'s studying in her room.*
(b) —Where's Kay?
   — She*'s in her room studying.*
	An expression of place can sometimes come between the auxiliary *be* and the *-ing* verb in a progressive tense, as in (b) and (d):
	   is + in her room + studying
	   was + in bed + reading

(c) —What was Jack doing when you arrived? — He *was reading* a book *in bed.*	In (a): The focus of both the question and the answer is on Kay's activity in progress, i.e., on what she is doing.
(d) —Where was Jack when you arrived? — He *was in bed reading* a book.	In (b): The focus of both the question and the answer is on Kay's location, i.e., on where Kay is.

CHAPTER 3
Perfect and Perfect Progressive Tenses

3-1 PRESENT PERFECT

(time?)	(a) They **have moved** into a new apartment. (b) **Have** you *ever* **visited** Mexico? (c) I **have** *never* **seen** snow. (d) I **have** *already* **seen** that movie. (e) Jack **hasn't seen** it *yet*. (f) Ann started a letter to her parents last week, but she *still* **hasn't finished** it. (g) Alex feels bad. He **has** *just* **heard** some bad news.	The present perfect expresses the idea that something happened (or never happened) *before now, at an unspecified time in the past*. The exact time it happened is not important. If there is a specific mention of time, the simple past is used: *They moved into a new apartment last month.* Notice in the examples: the adverbs ***ever, never, already, yet, still,*** and ***just*** are frequently used with the present perfect.
xxxx	(h) We **have had** four tests *so far* this semester. (i) I **have written** my wife a letter every other day *for* the last two weeks. (j) I **have met** many people *since* I came here in June. (k) I **have flown** on an airplane *many times*.	The present perfect also expresses the *repetition of an activity before now*. The exact time of each repetition is not important. Notice in (h): **so far** is frequently used with the present perfect.

	(l) I **have been** here *since seven o'clock*.
	(m) We **have been** here *for two weeks*.
	(n) I **have had** this same pair of shoes *for three years*.
	(o) I **have liked** cowboy movies ever *since I was a child*.
	(p) I **have known** him *for many years*.
		The present perfect, when used with ***for*** or ***since***, also expresses a situation that *began in the past and continues to the present.*
		In the examples, notice the difference between ***since*** and ***for***:
		    since + *a particular time*
		    for + *a duration of time*

*The verbs used in the present perfect to express a *situation* that began in the past and still exists are typically verbs with a stative meaning (see Chart 2-3, p. 8).
    The present perfect progressive, rather than the present perfect, is used with action verbs to express an *activity* that began in the past and continues to the present (see Chart 3-2, p. 18):
    I've been sitting at my desk for an hour. Jack has been watching TV since seven o'clock.

	Right now I am sitting at my desk. (a) I *have been sitting* here *since* seven o'clock. (b) I *have been sitting* here *for* two hours. (c) You *have been studying* for five straight hours. Why don't you take a break? (d) It *has been raining* all day. It is still raining right now.	This tense is used to indicate the *duration* of an activity that *began in the past and continues to the present.* When the tense has this meaning, it is used with time words, such as *for, since, all morning, all day, all week.*
	(e) I *have known* Alex since he was a child. (f) *INCORRECT*: I have been knowing Alex since he was a child.	Reminder: verbs with stative meanings are not used in the progressive. (See Chart 2-3, p. 8.) The present perfect, NOT the present perfect progressive, is used with stative verbs to describe the duration of a *state* (rather than an activity) that began in the past and continues to the present.
(recently)	(g) I *have been thinking* about changing my major. (h) All of the students *have been studying* hard. Final exams start next week. (i) My back hurts, so I *have been sleeping* on the floor lately. The bed is too soft.	When the tense is used without any specific mention of time, it expresses *a general activity in progress recently, lately.*
	(j) I *have lived* here since 1995. I *have been living* here since 1995. (k) He *has worked* at the same store for ten years. He *has been working* at the same store for ten years.	With certain verbs (most notably *live, work, teach)*, there is little or no difference in meaning between the two tenses when *since* or *for* is used.

Mr. Ford *has been waiting* in the dentist's office for 20 minutes.

3-3 PAST PERFECT

	(a) Sam *had* already *left* by the time Ann got there. (b) The thief simply walked in. Someone *had forgotten* to lock the door.	The past perfect expresses an activity that was *completed before another activity or time in the past.*
	(c) Sam *had* already *left* when Ann got there.	In (c): *First:* Sam left. *Second:* Ann got there.*
	(d) Sam *had left* before Ann got there. (e) Sam *left* before Ann got there. (f) *After* the guests *had left,* I went to bed. (g) *After* the guests *left,* I went to bed.	If either *before* or *after* is used in the sentence, the past perfect is often not necessary because the time relationship is already clear. The simple past may be used, as in (e) and (g). Note: (d) and (e) have the same meaning; (f) and (g) have the same meaning.

*COMPARE: *Sam **left** when Ann got there.* = First: *Ann got there.*
                                                       Second: *Sam left.*

3-4 PAST PERFECT PROGRESSIVE

	(a) The police *had been looking* for the criminal *for* two years before they caught him. (b) Eric finally came at six o'clock. I *had been waiting* for him *since* four-thirty.	The past perfect progressive emphasizes the *duration* of an activity that was *in progress before another activity or time in the past.*
	(c) When Judy got home, her hair was still wet because she *had been swimming.* (d) I went to Jane's house after the the funeral. Her eyes were red because she *had been crying.*	This tense also may express an activity *in progress close in time to another activity or time in the past.*

CHAPTER 4
Future Time

4-1 SIMPLE FUTURE: *WILL* AND *BE GOING TO*

	(a) Jack *will finish* his work tomorrow. (b) Jack *is going to finish* his work tomorrow. (c) Anna *will not be* here tomorrow. (d) Anna *won't be* here tomorrow.	*Will* or *be going to* is used to express future time.* In speech, *going to* is often pronounced "gonna." In (d): The contracted form of *will* + *not* is *won't*.

*The use of *shall* with *I* or *we* to express future time is possible but uncommon in American English. *Shall* is used more frequently in British English than in American English.

A: Why does he have an eraser in his hand?
B: He'*s going* to erase the board.

A: Who wants to erase the board?
   Are there any volunteers?
B: I'*ll* do it!
C: I'*ll* do it!

4-2 WILL vs. BE GOING TO

To express a PREDICTION: Use either *WILL* **or** *BE GOING TO*.

(a) According to the weather report, it ***will be*** cloudy tomorrow. (b) According to the weather report, it ***is going to be*** cloudy tomorrow. (c) Be careful! You***'ll hurt*** yourself! (d) Watch out! You***'re going to hurt*** yourself!	When the speaker is making a prediction (a statement about something s/he thinks will be true or will occur in the future), either ***will*** or ***be going to*** is possible. There is no difference in meaning between (a) and (b). There is no difference in meaning between (c) and (d).

To express a PRIOR PLAN: Use only *BE GOING TO*.

(e) A: Why did you buy this paint? B: I***'m going to paint*** my bedroom tomorrow. (f) I talked to Bob yesterday. He is tired of taking the bus to work. He***'s going to buy*** a car. That's what he told me.	When the speaker is expressing a prior plan (something the speaker intends to do in the future because in the past s/he has made a plan or decision to do it), only ***be going to*** is used.★ In (e): Speaker B has made a prior plan. Last week she decided to paint her bedroom. She intends to paint it tomorrow. In (f): The speaker knows Bob intends to buy a car. Bob made the decision in the past, and he plans to act on this decision in the future. ***Will*** is not appropriate in (e) and (f).

To express WILLINGNESS: Use only *WILL*.

(g) A: The phone's ringing.
     B: I***'ll get*** it.
 (h) A: I don't understand this problem.
     B: Ask your teacher about it. She***'ll help*** you.
	In (g): Speaker B is saying "I am willing; I am happy to get the phone." He is not making a prediction. He has made no prior plan to answer the phone. He is, instead, volunteering to answer the phone and uses ***will*** to show his willingness.
	 In (h): Speaker B feels sure about the teacher's willingness to help. ***Be going to*** is not appropriate in (g) and (h).

★COMPARE:

Situation 1: A: *Are you busy this evening?*

B: *Yes. **I'm going to meet** Jack at the library at seven. **We're going to study** together.*

In Situation 1, only ***be going to*** is possible. The speaker has a prior plan, so he uses ***be going to***.

Situation 2: A: *Are you busy this evening?*

B: *Well, I really haven't made any plans. **I'll eat** OR **I'm going to eat** dinner, of course. And then **I'll probably watch** OR **I'm probably going to watch** TV for a little while.*

In Situation 2, either ***will*** or ***be going to*** is possible. Speaker B has not planned his evening. He is "predicting" his evening (rather than stating any prior plans), so he may use either ***will*** or ***be going to***.

4-3 EXPRESSING THE FUTURE IN TIME CLAUSES

(a) Bob will come soon. *When Bob comes,* we will see him. (b) Linda is going to leave soon. *Before she leaves,* she is going to finish her work. (c) I will get home at 5:30. *After I get home,* I will eat dinner. (d) The taxi will arrive soon. *As soon as it arrives,* we'll be able to leave for the airport. (e) They are going to come soon. I'll wait here *until they come.*	In (a): *When Bob comes* is a time clause.★ *when* + *subject* + *verb* = *a time clause* *Will* or *be going to* is NOT used in a time clause. The meaning of the clause is future, but the **simple present** tense is used.

	A time clause begins with such words as *when, before, after, as soon as, until, while* and includes a subject and a verb. The time clause can come either at the beginning of the sentence or in the second part of the sentence:
	    When he comes, we'll see him. OR
	    We'll see him *when he comes.*

(f) *While I am traveling* in Europe next year, I'm going to save money by staying in youth hostels.	Sometimes the present progressive is used in a time clause to express an activity that will be in progress in the future, as in (f).
(g) I will go to bed *after I finish* my work. (h) I will go to bed *after I have finished* my work.	Occasionally, the present perfect is used in a time clause, as in (h). Examples (g) and (h) have the same meaning. The present perfect in the time clause emphasizes the completion of the act before the other act occurs in the future.

★A "time clause" is an adverb clause. See Charts 5-1 (p. 24), 5-2 (p. 25), and 17-1 (p. 88) for more information.

4-4 USING THE PRESENT PROGRESSIVE AND THE SIMPLE PRESENT TO EXPRESS FUTURE TIME

PRESENT PROGRESSIVE (a) My wife has an appointment with a doctor. She *is seeing* Dr. North *next Tuesday.* (b) Sam has already made his plans. He *is leaving* at *noon tomorrow.* (c) A: What are you going to do this afternoon? B: *After lunch* I *am meeting* a friend of mine. We *are going* shopping. Would you like to come along?	The present progressive may be used to express future time when the idea of the sentence concerns a planned event or definite intention. (COMPARE: A verb such as *rain* is not used in the present progressive to indicate future time because rain is not a planned event.) A future meaning for the present progressive tense is indicated either by future time words in the sentence or by the context.
SIMPLE PRESENT (d) The museum *opens* at ten tomorrow morning. (e) Classes *begin* next week. (f) John's plane *arrives* at 6:05 P.M. next Monday.	The simple present can also be used to express future time in a sentence concerning events that are on a definite schedule or timetable. These sentences usually contain future time words. Only a few verbs are used in this way: e.g., *open, close, begin, end, start, finish, arrive, leave, come, return.*

4-5 FUTURE PROGRESSIVE

	(a) I will begin to study at seven. You will come at eight. I *will be studying* when you come. (b) Right now I am sitting in class. At this same time tomorrow, I *will be sitting* in class.	The future progressive expresses an activity that will *be in progress at a time in the future.*
	(c) Don't call me at nine because I won't be home. I *am going to be studying* at the library.	The progressive form of *be going to:* *be going to + be + -ing*
	(d) Don't get impatient. She *will be coming* soon. (e) Don't get impatient. She *will come* soon.	Sometimes there is little or no difference between the future progressive and the simple future, especially when the future event will occur at an indefinite time in the future, as in (d) and (e).

4-6 FUTURE PERFECT

	(a) I will graduate in June. I will see you in July. By the time I see you, I *will have graduated*. (b) I *will have finished* my homework by the time I go out on a date tonight.	The future perfect expresses an activity that will be *completed before another time or event in the future.* (Note: *by the time* introduces a time clause; the simple present is used in a time clause.)

4-7 FUTURE PERFECT PROGRESSIVE

	(c) I will go to bed at ten P.M. Ed will get home at midnight. At midnight I will be sleeping. I *will have been sleeping* for two hours by the time Ed gets home.	The future perfect progressive emphasizes the *duration* of an activity that will be *in progress before another time or event in the future.*
	(d) When Professor Jones retires next month, he *will have taught* for 45 years. (e) When Professor Jones retires next month, he *will have been teaching* for 45 years.	Sometimes the future perfect and the future perfect progressive have the same meaning, as in (d) and (e). Also, notice that the activity expressed by either of these two tenses may begin in the past.

5-1 ADVERB CLAUSES OF TIME: FORM

adverb clause ⌐————⌐ main clause ⌐————⌐ (a) **_When the phone rang,_** the baby woke up.	In (a): **_When the phone rang_** is an adverb clause of time. An adverb clause is one kind of dependent clause. A dependent clause must be attached to an independent, or main, clause. In (a): **_the baby woke up_** is the main clause.
(b) INCORRECT: When the phone rang. The baby woke up. (c) The phone rang. The baby woke up.	Example (b) is incorrect because the adverb clause is not connected to the main clause. Example (c) is correct because there is no adverb clause. The two main clauses are both independent sentences.
(d) **_When the phone rang,_** the baby woke up. (e) The baby woke up **_when the phone rang_**.	Examples (d) and (e) have the same meaning. An adverb clause can come in front of a main clause, as in (d), or follow the main clause, as in (e). Notice that a comma is used to separate the two clauses when the adverb clause comes first.

When Jennifer went for a ride yesterday, she fell off her horse.

5-2 USING ADVERB CLAUSES TO SHOW TIME RELATIONSHIPS

after*	(a) *After she graduates,* she will get a job. (b) *After she (had) graduated,* she got a job.	A present tense, NOT a future tense, is used in an adverb clause of time, as in examples (a) and (c). (See Chart 4-3, p. 22, for tense usage in future time clauses.)
before*	(c) I will leave *before he comes.* (d) I (had) left *before he came.*	
when	(e) *When I arrived,* he *was talking* on the phone. (f) *When I got there,* he *had* already *left.* (g) *When it began to rain,* I *stood* under a tree. (h) *When I was in Chicago,* I *visited* the museums. (i) *When I see him tomorrow,* I *will ask* him.	*when* = at that time Notice the different time relationships expressed by the tenses.
while as	(j) *While I was walking home,* it began to rain. (k) *As I was walking home,* it began to rain.	*while, as* = during that time
by the time	(l) *By the time he arrived,* we *had* already *left.* (m) *By the time he comes,* we *will have* already *left.*	*by the time* = one event is completed before another event Notice the use of the past perfect and future perfect in the main clause.
since	(n) I *haven't seen* him *since he left this morning.* (o) I*'ve known* her *ever since I was a child.*	*since* = from that time to the present In (o): *ever* adds emphasis. Note: The present perfect is used in the main clause.
until till	(p) We stayed there *until we finished our work.* (q) We stayed there *till we finished our work.*	*until, till* = to that time and then no longer (*Till* is used more in speaking than in writing; it is generally not used in formal English.)
as soon as once	(r) *As soon as it stops raining,* we will leave. (s) *Once it stops raining,* we will leave.	*as soon as, once* = when one event happens, another event happens soon afterward
as long as so long as	(t) I will never speak to him again *as long as I live.* (u) I will never speak to him again *so long as I live.*	*as long as, so long as* = during all that time, from beginning to end
whenever every time	(v) *Whenever I see her,* I say hello. (w) *Every time I see her,* I say hello.	*whenever* = every time
the first time the last time the next time	(x) *The first time (that) I went to New York,* I went to an opera. (y) I saw two plays *the last time (that) I went to New York.* (z) *The next time (that) I go to New York,* I'm going to see a ballet.	Adverb clauses can be introduced by the following: *the* { *first* *second* *third, etc.* *last* *next* *etc.* } *time (that)*

*After and before are commonly used in the following expressions:

shortly *after*   **shortly** *before*
a short time *after*   **a short time** *before*
a little while *after*   **a little while** *before*
not long *after*   **not long** *before*
soon *after*

CHAPTER **6**
Subject–Verb Agreement

6-1 FINAL -*S/-ES:* USE, PRONUNCIATION, AND SPELLING

(a) NOUN + *-s:* *Friends* are important.
NOUN + *-es:* I like my *classes.*
	A final *-s* or *-es* is added to a noun to make the noun plural.
	    friend = *a singular noun*
	    friends = *a plural noun*

(b) VERB + *-s:* Mary *works* at the bank. VERB + *-es:* John *watches* birds.	A final *-s* or *-es* is added to a simple present verb when the subject is a singular noun (e.g., *Mary, my father, the machine*) or third person singular pronoun *(she, he, it).* **Mary works** = *singular* **She works** = *singular* **The students work** = *plural* **They work** = *plural*

PRONUNCIATION OF -*S/-ES*

(c) seats → *seat*/s/ ropes → *rope*/s/ backs → *back*/s/	Final *-s* is pronounced /s/ after voiceless sounds, as in (c): "t," "p," and "k" are examples of voiceless sounds.*
(d) seeds → *seed*/z/ robes → *robe*/z/ bags → *bag*/z/ sees → *see*/z/	Final *-s* is pronounced /z/ after voiced sounds, as in (h): "d," "b," "g," and "ee" are examples of voiced sounds.*
(e) dishes → *dish*/əz/ catches → *catch*/əz/ kisses → *kiss*/əz/ mixes → *mix*/əz/ prizes → *prize*/əz/ edges → *edge*/əz/	Final *-s* and *-es* are pronounced /əz/ after "-sh," "-ch," "-s," "-z," and "-ge"/"-dge" sounds. The /əz/ ending adds a syllable. All of the words in (e) are pronounced with two syllables. COMPARE: All of the words in (c) and (d) are pronounced with one syllable.

SPELLING: FINAL -*S* vs. -*ES*

(f) sing → *sings* song → *songs*	For most words (whether a verb or a noun), simply a final *-s* is added to spell the word correctly.
(g) wash → *washes* watch → *watches* class → *classes* buzz → *buzzes* box → *boxes*	Final *-es* is added to words that end in *-sh, -ch, -s, -z,* and *-x.*
(h) toy → *toys* buy → *buys* (i) baby → *babies* cry → *cries*	For words that end in *-y:* In (h): If *-y* is preceded by a vowel, only *-s* is added. In (i): If *-y* is preceded by a consonant, the *-y* is changed to *-i* and *-es* is added.

*See Chart 2-6, p. 11, for an explanation of voiced vs. voiceless sounds.

6-2 BASIC SUBJECT–VERB AGREEMENT

SINGULAR VERB	PLURAL VERB	
(a) My *friend* **lives** in Boston.	(b) My *friends* **live** in Boston.	*verb* + **-s/-es** = third person singular in the simple present tense *noun* + **-s/-es** = plural
	(c) My *brother* **and** *sister* **live** in Boston. (d) My *brother, sister,* **and** *cousin* **live** in Boston.	Two or more subjects connected by **and** require a plural verb.
(e) **Every** *man, woman,* **and** *child* **needs** love. (f) **Each** *book* **and** *magazine* **is** listed in the card catalog.		EXCEPTION: **Every** and **each** are always followed immediately by singular nouns. (See Chart 7-13, p. 37.) In this case, even when there are two (or more) nouns connected by **and,** the verb is singular.
(g) That *book* on political parties *is* interesting. (i) My *dog,* as well as my cats, **likes** cat food. (k) The *book* that I got from my parents *was* very interesting.	(h) The *ideas* in that book **are** interesting. (j) My *dogs,* as well as my cat, **like** cat food. (l) The *books* I bought at the bookstore **were** expensive.	Sometimes a phrase or clause separates a subject from its verb. These interrupting structures do not affect basic agreement. For example, in (g) the interrupting prepositional phrase **on political parties** does not change the fact that the verb **is** must agree with the subject **book**. In (k) and (l): The subject and verb are separated by an adjective clause. (See Chapter 13.)
(m) *Growing* flowers *is* her hobby.		A gerund used as the subject of the sentence requires a singular verb. (See Chart 14-11, p. 81.)

Annie had a hard time when she was coming home
from the store because the *bag* of groceries **was**
too heavy for her to carry.

6-3 SUBJECT–VERB AGREEMENT: USING EXPRESSIONS OF QUANTITY

SINGULAR VERB	PLURAL VERB	
(a) *Some of the **book is** good.*	(b) *Some of the **books are** good.*	In most expressions of quantity, the verb is determined by the noun (or pronoun) that follows ***of***. For example: In (a): ***Some of*** + *singular noun = singular verb.* In (b): ***Some of*** + *plural noun = plural verb.*
(c) *A lot of the **equipment is** new.*	(d) *A lot of my **friends are** here.*	
(e) *Two-thirds of the **money is** mine.*	(f) *Two-thirds of the **pennies are** mine.*	

(g) ***One** of my friends **is** here.*
(h) ***Each** of my friends **is** here.*
(i) ***Every one** of my friends **is** here.*
		EXCEPTIONS: ***One of, each of***, and ***every one of*** take singular verbs.
		    one of
		    each of + *plural noun = singular verb*
		    every one of

(j) ***None** of the boys **is** here.*	(k) ***None** of the boys **are** here.* (informal)	Subjects with ***none of*** are considered singular in very formal English, but plural verbs are often used in informal speech writing.
(l) ***The number** of students in the class **is** fifteen.*	(m) ***A number** of students **were** late for class.*	COMPARE: In (l): ***The number*** is the subject. In (m): ***A number of*** is an expression of quantity meaning "a lot of." It is followed by a plural noun and a plural verb.

6-4 SUBJECT–VERB AGREEMENT: USING *THERE* + *BE*

(a) ***There are** twenty students in my class.* (b) ***There's** a fly in the room.*	In the structure ***there + be***, *there* is called an "expletive." It has no meaning as a vocabulary word. It introduces the idea that something exists in a particular place. Pattern: ***there + be** + subject + expression of place*
(c) ***There are** seven continents.*	Sometimes the expression of place is omitted when the meaning is clear. In (c): The implied expression of place is clearly *in the world*.

SINGULAR VERB	PLURAL VERB	
(d) There *is a book* on the shelf.	(e) There ***are** some books* on the shelf.	The subject follows ***be*** when ***there*** is used. In (d): The subject is *book*. In (e): The subject is *books*.
(f) INFORMAL: There***'s** some books* on the shelf.		In very informal spoken English, some native speakers use a singular verb even when the subject is plural, as in (f). The use of this form is fairly frequent but is not generally considered to be grammatically correct.

SINGULAR VERB	
(a) *The United States* **is** big. (b) *The Philippines* **consists** of more than 7,000 islands. (c) *The United Nations* **has** its headquarters in New York City. (d) *Sears* **is** a department store.	Sometimes a proper noun that ends in **-s** is singular. In the examples, if the noun is changed to a pronoun, the singular pronoun **it** is used (not the plural pronoun **they**) because the noun is singular. In (a): **The United States** = **it** (not **they**).
(e) The *news* **is** interesting.	**News** is singular.
(f) *Mathematics* **is** easy for her. *Physics* **is** easy for her too.	Fields of study that end in **-ics** require singular verbs.
(g) *Diabetes* **is** an illness.	Certain illnesses that end in **-s** are singular: *diabetes, measles, mumps, rabies, rickets, shingles.*
(h) *Eight hours* of sleep **is** enough. (i) *Ten dollars* **is** too much to pay. (j) *Five thousand miles* **is** too far to travel.	Expressions of *time, money,* and *distance* usually require a singular verb.

(k) *Two and two* **is** four.
   Two and two **equals** four.
   Two plus two **is/equals** four.
(l) *Five times five* **is** twenty-five.
	Arithmetic expressions require singular verbs.

PLURAL VERB	
(m) *Those people* **are** from Canada. (n) *The police* **have** been called. (o) *Cattle* **are** domestic animals.	**People,* police,** and **cattle** do not end in **-s,** but are plural nouns and require plural verbs.

SINGULAR VERB	PLURAL VERB	
(p) *English* **is** spoken in many countries. (r) *Chinese* **is** his native language.	(q) *The English* **drink** tea. (s) *The Chinese* **have** an interesting history.	In (p): **English** = language. In (q): **The English** = people from England. Some nouns of nationality that end in **-sh, -ese,** and **-ch** can mean either language or people, e.g., *English, Spanish, Chinese, Japanese, Vietnamese, Portuguese, French.*
	(t) *The poor* **have** many problems. (u) *The rich* **get** richer.	A few adjectives can be preceded by **the** and used as a plural noun (without final **-s**) to refer to people who have that quality. Other examples: *the young, the elderly, the living, the dead, the blind, the deaf, the disabled.*

*The word "people" has a final **-s** (*peoples*) only when it is used to refer to ethnic or national groups: *All the peoples of the world desire peace.*

CHAPTER 7
Nouns

7-1 REGULAR AND IRREGULAR PLURAL NOUNS

(a) *song–songs*	The plural of most nouns is formed by adding final *-s*.*
(b) *box–boxes*	Final *-es* is added to nouns that end in *-sh*, *-ch*, *-s*, *-z*, and *-x*.*
(c) *baby–babies*	The plural of words that end in a consonant + *-y* is spelled *-ies*.*
(d) *man–men* *ox–oxen* *tooth–teeth* *woman–women* *foot–feet* *mouse–mice* *child–children* *goose–geese* *louse–lice*	The nouns in (d) have irregular plural forms that do not end in *-s*.
(e) *echo–echoes* *potato–potatoes* *hero–heroes* *tomato–tomatoes*	Some nouns that end in *-o* add *-es* to form the plural.
(f) *auto–autos* *photo–photos* *studio–studios* *ghetto–ghettos* *piano–pianos* *tatoo–tatoos* *kangaroo–kangaroos* *radio–radios* *video–videos* *kilo–kilos* *solo–solos* *zoo–zoos* *memo–memos* *soprano–sopranos*	Some nouns that end in *-o* add only *-s* to form the plural.
(g) *memento–mementoes/mementos* *volcano–volcanoes/volcanos* *mosquito–mosquitoes/mosquitos* *zero–zeroes/zeros* *tornado–tornadoes/tornados*	Some nouns that end in *-o* add either *-es* or *-s* to form the plural (with *-es* being the more usual plural form).
(h) *calf–calves* *life–lives* *thief–thieves* *half–halves* *loaf–loaves* *wolf–wolves* *knife–knives* *self–selves* *scarf–scarves/scarfs* *leaf–leaves* *shelf–shelves*	Some nouns that end in *-f* or *-fe* are changed to *-ves* to form the plural.
(i) *belief–beliefs* *cliff–cliffs* *chief–chiefs* *roof–roofs*	Some nouns that end in *-f* simply add *-s* to form the plural.
(j) *one deer–two deer* *one series–two series* *one fish–two fish*** *one sheep–two sheep* *one means–two means* *one shrimp–two shrimp**** *one offspring–two offspring* *one species–two species*	Some nouns have the same singular and plural form: e.g., *One deer is . . . . Two deer are . . . .*

(k) *criterion–criteria*   (o) *analysis–analyses*
    phenomenon–phenomena   *basis–bases*
                    crisis–crises
(l) *cactus–cacti/cactuses*   *hypothesis–hypotheses*
    fungus–fungi   *oasis–oases*
    nucleus–nuclei   *parenthesis–parentheses*
    stimulus–stimuli   *thesis–theses*
    syllabus–syllabi/syllabuses
(m) *formula–formulae/formulas*   (p) *bacterium–bacteria*
    vertebra–vertebrae   *curriculum–curricula*
                    datum–data
(n) *appendix–appendices/appendixes*   *medium–media*
    index–indices/indexes   *memorandum–memoranda*
	Some nouns that English has borrowed from other languages have foreign plurals.

*For information about the pronunciation and spelling of words ending in *-s/-es*, see Chart 6-1, p. 26.
**Fishes is also possible, but rarely used.
***Especially in British English, but also occasionally in American English, the plural of *shrimp* can be *shrimps*.

7-2 POSSESSIVE NOUNS

SINGULAR NOUN	POSSESSIVE FORM	To show possession, add an apostrophe (') and *-s* to a singular noun: The ***girl's*** book is on the table.
(a) *the girl*	***the girl's***	
(b) *Tom*	***Tom's***	If a singular noun ends in *-s*, there are two possible forms:
(c) *my wife*	***my wife's***	1. Add an apostrophe and *-s*: ***Thomas's*** book.
(d) *a lady*	***a lady's***	2. Add only an apostrophe: ***Thomas'*** book.
(e) *Thomas*	***Thomas's/Thomas'***	
PLURAL NOUN	POSSESSIVE FORM	Add only an apostrophe to a plural noun that ends in *-s*: The ***girls'*** books are on the table.
(f) *the girls*	***the girls'***	
(g) *their wives*	***their wives'***	
(h) *the ladies*	***the ladies'***	
(i) *the men*	***the men's***	Add an apostrophe and *-s* to plural nouns that do not end in *-s*: The ***men's*** books are on the table.
(j) *my children*	***my children's***	

7-3 USING NOUNS AS MODIFIERS

(a)	The soup has vegetables in it. It is ***vegetable soup***.	When a noun is used as a modifier, it is in its singular form.* In (a): ***vegetable*** modifies ***soup***.
(b)	The building has offices in it. It is an ***office building***.	In (b): ***office*** modifies ***building***.
(c)	The test lasted two hours. It was a ***two-hour test***.	When a noun used as a modifier is combined with a number expression, the noun is singular and a hyphen (-) is used. INCORRECT: She has a *five years old* son.
(d)	Her son is five years old. She has a ***five-year-old son***.	

*Adjectives never take a final *-s*. (INCORRECT: *beautifuls pictures*) See Appendix Chart A-3, p. A2. Similarly, nouns used as adjectives never take a final *-s*. (INCORRECT: *vegetables soup*)

Harry's bed has a ***mosquito net***.

7-4 COUNT AND NONCOUNT NOUNS

(a) I bought *a chair*. Sam bought *three chairs*.
(b) We bought *some furniture*.
    INCORRECT: We bought some *furnitures*.
    INCORRECT: We bought a *furniture*.
			Chair is a count noun; chairs are items that can be counted.
			Furniture is a noncount noun. In grammar, furniture cannot be counted.

	SINGULAR	PLURAL	
COUNT NOUN	*a* chair *one* chair	Ø chairs★ *two* chairs *some* chairs *a lot of* chairs *many* chairs	A count noun: (1) may be preceded by *a/an* in the singular. (2) takes a final *-s/-es* in the plural.
NONCOUNT NOUN	Ø furniture★ *some* furniture *a lot of* furniture *much* furniture		A noncount noun: (1) is not immediately preceded by *a/an*. (2) has no plural form, so does not take a final *-s/-es*.

★Ø = nothing.

7-5 NONCOUNT NOUNS

(a) I bought some chairs, tables, and desks. In other words, I bought some *furniture*. (b) I put some *sugar* in my *coffee*.	Many noncount nouns refer to a "whole" that is made up of different parts. In (a): *furniture* represents a whole group of things that is made up of similar but separate items. In (b): *sugar* and *coffee* represent whole masses made up of individual particles or elements.★
(c) I wish you *luck*.	Many noncount nouns are abstractions. In (c): *luck* is an abstract concept, an abstract "whole." It has no physical form; you can't touch it. You can't count it.
(d) *Sunshine* is warm and cheerful.	A phenomenon of nature, such as *sunshine,* is frequently used as a noncount noun, as in (d).

(e) NONCOUNT: Ann has brown *hair*.
        COUNT: Tom has a *hair* on his jacket.
(f) NONCOUNT: I opened the curtains to let in some *light*.
        COUNT: Don't forget to turn off the *light* before you go to bed.
	Many nouns can be used as either noncount or count nouns, but the meaning is different; e.g., *hair* in (e) and *light* in (f).
	(Dictionaries written especially for learners of English as a second language are a good source of information on count/noncount usages of nouns.)

★To express a particular quantity, some noncount nouns may be preceded by unit expressions: *a spoonful of sugar, a glass of water, a cup of coffee, a quart of milk, a loaf of bread, a grain of rice, a bowl of soup, a bag of flour, a pound of meat, a piece of furniture, a piece of paper, a piece of jewelry.*

7-6 SOME COMMON NONCOUNT NOUNS

This list is a sample of nouns that are commonly used as noncount nouns. Many other nouns can also be used as noncount nouns.

(a) WHOLE GROUPS MADE UP OF SIMILAR ITEMS: *baggage, clothing, equipment, food, fruit, furniture, garbage, hardware, jewelry, junk, luggage, machinery, mail, makeup, money/cash/change, postage, scenery, traffic, etc.*

(b) FLUIDS: *water, coffee, tea, milk, oil, soup, gasoline, blood, etc.*

(c) SOLIDS: *ice, bread, butter, cheese, meat, gold, iron, silver, glass, paper, wood, cotton, wool, etc.*

(d) GASES: *steam, air, oxygen, nitrogen, smoke, smog, pollution, etc.*

(e) PARTICLES: *rice, chalk, corn, dirt, dust, flour, grass, hair, pepper, salt, sand, sugar, wheat, etc.*

(f) ABSTRACTIONS:
—*beauty, confidence, courage, education, enjoyment, fun, happiness, health, help, honesty, hospitality, importance, intelligence, justice, knowledge, laughter, luck, music, patience, peace, pride, progress, recreation, significance, sleep, truth, violence, wealth, etc.*
—*advice, information, news, evidence, proof, etc.*
—*time, space, energy, etc.*
—*homework, work, etc.*
—*grammar, slang, vocabulary, etc.*

(g) LANGUAGES: *Arabic, Chinese, English, Spanish, etc.*

(h) FIELDS OF STUDY: *chemistry, engineering, history, literature, mathematics, psychology, etc.*

(i) RECREATION: *baseball, soccer, tennis, chess, bridge, poker, etc.*

(j) ACTIVITIES: *driving, studying, swimming, traveling,* walking, etc.* (and other gerunds)

(k) NATURAL PHENOMENA: *weather, dew, fog, hail, heat, humidity, lightning, rain, sleet, snow, thunder, wind, darkness, light, sunshine, electricity, fire, gravity, etc.*

*British spelling: *travelling.*

This yard is full of *junk*.

7-7 BASIC ARTICLE USAGE

I. USING *A* or Ø: GENERIC NOUNS

SINGULAR COUNT NOUN	(a) ***A banana*** is yellow.*	A speaker uses generic nouns to make generalizations. A generic noun represents a whole class of things; it is not a specific, real, concrete thing, but rather a symbol of a whole group.
PLURAL COUNT NOUN	(b) **Ø** *Bananas* are yellow.	In (a) and (b): The speaker is talking about any banana, all bananas, bananas in general. In (c): The speaker is talking about any and all fruit, fruit in general.
NONCOUNT NOUN	(c) **Ø** *Fruit* is good for you.	Notice that no article (Ø) is used to make generalizations with plural count nouns, as in (b), and with noncount nouns, as in (c).

II. USING *A* or *SOME:* INDEFINITE NOUNS

SINGULAR COUNT NOUN	(d) I ate ***a banana***.	Indefinite nouns are actual things (not symbols), but they are not specifically identified.
PLURAL COUNT NOUN	(e) I ate ***some*** *bananas*.	In (d): The speaker is not referring to "this banana" or "that banana" or "the banana you gave me." The speaker is simply saying that s/he ate one banana. The listener does not know nor need to know which specific banana was eaten; it was simply one banana out of that whole group of things in this world called bananas.
NONCOUNT NOUN	(f) I ate ***some*** *fruit*.	In (e) and (f): ***Some*** is often used with indefinite plural count nouns and indefinite noncount nouns. In addition to ***some***, a speaker might use *two*, ***a few***, ***several***, ***a lot of***, *etc.*, with plural count nouns, or ***a little***, ***a lot of***, *etc.*, with noncount nouns. (See Chart 7-4, p. 32.)

III. USING *THE:* DEFINITE NOUNS

SINGULAR COUNT NOUN	(g) Thank you for ***the*** *banana*.	A noun is definite when both the speaker and the listener are thinking about the same specific thing.
PLURAL COUNT NOUN	(h) Thank you for ***the*** *bananas*.	In (g): The speaker uses ***the*** because the listener knows which specific banana the speaker is talking about, i.e., that particular banana which the listener gave to the speaker.
NONCOUNT NOUN	(i) Thank you for ***the*** *fruit*.	Notice that ***the*** is used with both singular and plural count nouns and with noncount nouns.

*Usually *a/an* is used with a singular generic count noun. Examples:
> ***A window*** *is made of glass.* ***A doctor*** *heals sick people.* *Parents must give* ***a child*** *love.* ***A box*** *has six sides.* ***An apple*** *can be red, green, or yellow.*

However, ***the*** is sometimes used with a singular generic count noun (not a plural generic count noun, not a generic noncount noun). "Generic ***the***" is commonly used with, in particular:

(1) species of animals: ***The blue whale*** *is the largest mammal on earth.*
> ***The elephant*** *is the largest land mammal.*

(2) inventions: *Who invented* ***the telephone?*** ***the wheel?*** ***the refrigerator?*** ***the airplane?***
> ***The computer*** *will play an increasingly large role in all of our lives.*

(3) musical instruments: *I'd like to learn to play* ***the piano***.
> *Do you play* ***the guitar?***

7-8 GENERAL GUIDELINES FOR ARTICLE USAGE

(a) *The sun* is bright today. Please hand this book to *the teacher*. Please open *the door*. Omar is in *the kitchen*.	GUIDELINE: Use *the* when you know or assume that your listener is familiar with and thinking about the same specific thing or person you are talking about.
(b) Yesterday I saw *some dogs*. *The dogs* were chasing *a cat*. *The cat* was chasing *a mouse*. *The mouse* ran into *a hole*. *The hole* was very small.	GUIDELINE: Use *the* for the second mention of an indefinite noun.* In (b): first mention = *some dogs, a cat, a mouse, a hole;* second mention = *the dogs, the cat, the mouse, the hole.*
(c) CORRECT: *Apples* are my favorite fruit. INCORRECT: The apples are my favorite fruit. (d) CORRECT: *Gold* is a metal. INCORRECT: The gold is a metal.	GUIDELINE: Do NOT use *the* with a plural count noun (e.g., *apples*) or a noncount noun (e.g., *gold*) when you are making a generalization.
(e) CORRECT: (1) I drove *a car*. / I drove *the car*. 　　　　　(2) I drove *that car*. 　　　　　(3) I drove *his car*. INCORRECT: I drove *car*.	GUIDELINE: A singular count noun (e.g., *car*) is always preceded by: (1) an article (*a/an* or *the*); OR (2) *this/that*; OR (3) a possessive pronoun.

*___The___ is not used for the second mention of a generic noun. COMPARE:
(1) *What color is* ___a banana___ (generic noun)? ___A banana___ (generic noun) *is yellow.*
(2) *Joe offered me* ___a banana___ (indefinite noun) *or an apple. I chose* ___the banana___ (definite noun).

7-9 EXPRESSIONS OF QUANTITY

EXPRESSIONS OF QUANTITY	USED WITH COUNT NOUNS	USED WITH NONCOUNT NOUNS	An expression of quantity may precede a noun. Some expressions of quantity are used only with count nouns, as in (a) and (b).
(a) *one* *each* *every*	*one apple* *each apple* *every apple*	Ø* Ø Ø	
(b) *two, etc.* *both* *a couple of* *a few* *several* *many* *a number of*	*two apples* *both apples* *a couple of apples* *a few apples* *several apples* *many apples* *a number of apples*	Ø Ø Ø Ø Ø Ø	
(c) *a little* *much* *a great deal of*	Ø Ø Ø	*a little rice* *much rice* *a great deal of rice*	Some are used only with noncount nouns, as in (c).
(d) *no* *some/any* *a lot of/lots of* *plenty of* *most* *all*	*no apples* *some/any apples* *a lot of/lots of apples* *plenty of apples* *most apples* *all apples*	*no rice* *some/any rice* *a lot of/lots of rice* *plenty of rice* *most rice* *all rice*	Some are used with both count and noncount nouns, as in (d).

*Ø = not used. For example, you can say *"I ate one apple"* but NOT *"I ate one rice."*

7-10 USING *A FEW* AND *FEW; A LITTLE* AND *LITTLE*

a few
 	
a little
	(a) She has been here only two weeks, but she has already made **a few friends**.
	   (Positive idea: *She has made some friends.*)
	(b) I'm very pleased. I've been able to save **a little money** this month.
	   (Positive idea: *I have saved some money instead of spending all of it.*)
		A few and **a little*** give a positive idea; they indicate that something exists, is present, as in (a) and (b).

few
 	
little
	(c) I feel sorry for her. She has **(very) few friends**.
	   (Negative idea: *She does not have many friends; she has almost no friends.*)
	(d) I have **(very) little money**. I don't even have enough money to buy food for dinner.
	   (Negative idea: *I do not have much money; I have almost no money.*)
		Few and **little** (without **a**) give a negative idea; they indicate that something is largely absent.
		
		Very (+ **few**/**little**) makes the negative stronger, the number/amount smaller.

*A few and **few** are used with plural count nouns. **A little** and **little** are used with noncount nouns.

7-11 USING *OF* IN EXPRESSIONS OF QUANTITY

(a) CORRECT: **A lot of books** are paperbacks. (b) CORRECT: **A lot of my books** are paperbacks. (c) INCORRECT: A lot books are paperbacks.	Some expressions of quantity (such as *a lot of*) always contain **of**, as in (a) and (b). See GROUP ONE below.
(d) CORRECT: **Many of my books** are paperbacks. (e) INCORRECT: Many my books are paperbacks. (f) CORRECT: **Many books** are paperbacks. (g) INCORRECT: Many of books are paperbacks.	Sometimes **of** is used with an expression of quantity, as in (d), and sometimes **of** is NOT used with the same expression of quantity, as in (f). See GROUP TWO below.

GROUP ONE: EXPRESSIONS OF QUANTITY THAT ALWAYS CONTAIN *OF*

a lot **of**	*a number* **of**	*a majority* **of**
lots **of**	*a great deal* **of**	*plenty* **of**

GROUP TWO: EXPRESSIONS OF QUANTITY THAT SOMETIMES CONTAIN *OF* AND SOMETIMES NOT

all (of)	*many (of)*	*one (of)*	*both (of)*	*some (of)*
most (of)	*much (of)*	*two (of)*	*several (of)*	*any (of)*
almost all (of)	*a few (of)*	*three (of)*		
	a little (of)	*etc.*		

(h) *Many* **of my** *books* are in English.
(i) *Many* **of those** *books* are in English.
(j) *Many* **of the** *books* on that shelf are in English.
	Of is used with the expressions of quantity in GROUP TWO when the noun is specific. A noun is specific when it is preceded by:
	   1. *my, John's* (or any possessive), as in (h).
	   2. *this, that, these,* or *those,* as in (i).
	   3. *the,* as in (j)

(k) **Many books** are in English.	**Of** is NOT used with the expressions of quantity in GROUP TWO if the noun it modifies is *nonspecific*. In (k): The noun **books** is nonspecific; ie., the speaker is not referring to "your books" or "these books" or "the books on that desk." The speaker is not referring to specific books, but to books in general.

7-12 *ALL (OF)* AND *BOTH (OF)*

(a) CORRECT: *All of the students* in my class are here. (b) CORRECT: *All the students* in my class are here.	When a noun is specific (e.g., *the students*), using *of* after *all* is optional as in (a) and (b).
(c) CORRECT: *All students* must have an I.D. card. (d) *INCORRECT: All of students* must have an I.D. card.	When a noun is nonspecific, *of* does NOT follow *all*, as in (c).
(e) I know *both (of) those men*.	Similarly, using *of* after *both* is optional when the noun is specific, as in (e).
(f) CORRECT: I know *both men*. (g) *INCORRECT:* I know *both of men*.	When a noun is nonspecific, *of* does NOT follow *both*, as in (f).

7-13 SINGULAR EXPRESSIONS OF QUANTITY: *ONE, EACH, EVERY*

(a) *One student* was late to class. (b) *Each student* has a schedule. (c) *Every student* has a schedule.	*One*, *each*, and *every* are followed immediately by *singular count nouns* (never plural nouns, never noncount nouns).
(d) *One of the students* was late to class. (e) *Each (one) of the students* has a schedule. (f) *Every one of the students* has a schedule.	*One of*, *each of*, and *every one of*★ are followed by *specific plural count nouns* (never singular nouns; never noncount nouns).

★COMPARE:

Every one (two words) is an expression of quantity; e.g., *I have read **every one** of those books.*

Everyone (one word) is an indefinite pronoun; it has the same meaning as *everybody*; e.g., *Everyone/Everybody* has a schedule.

NOTE: *Each* and *every* have essentially the same meaning.

Each is used when the speaker is thinking of one person/thing at a time: *Each student has a schedule. = Mary has a schedule. Hiroshi has a schedule. Carlos has a schedule. Sabrina has a schedule. (etc.)*

Every is used when the speaker means "all": *Every student has a schedule. = All of the students have schedules.*

CHAPTER 8
Pronouns

8-1 PERSONAL PRONOUNS

	SUBJECT PRONOUN	OBJECT PRONOUN	POSSESSIVE PRONOUN	POSSESSIVE ADJECTIVE
SINGULAR	*I* *you* *she, he, it*	*me* *you* *her, him, it*	*mine* *your* *hers, his, its*	*my* name *your* name *her, his, its* name
PLURAL	*we* *you* *they*	*us* *you* *them*	*ours* *yours* *theirs*	*our* names *your* names *their* names

(a) I read *a book*. *It* was good. (b) I read *some books*. *They* were good.	A pronoun is used in place of a noun. The noun it refers to is called the "antecedent." In (a): The pronoun *it* refers to the antecedent noun *book*. A singular pronoun is used to refer to a singular noun, as in (a). A plural pronoun is used to refer to a plural noun, as in (b).
(c) *I* like tea. Do *you* like tea too?	Sometimes the antecedent noun is understood, not explicitly stated. In (c): *I* refers to the speaker, and *you* refers to the person the speaker is talking to.
(d) John has a car. *He drives* to work.	Subject pronouns are used as subjects of sentences, as *he* in (d).
(e) John works in my office. I *know him* well. (f) I talk *to him* every day.	Object pronouns are used as the objects of verbs, as in (e), or as the objects of prepositions, as in (f).
(g) That book is *hers*. *Yours* is over there. (h) *INCORRECT:* That book is *her's*. *Your's* is over there.	Possessive pronouns are not followed immediately by a noun; they stand alone, as in (g). In (h): Possessive pronouns do NOT take apostrophes. (See Chart 7-2, p. 31, for the use of apostrophes with possessive nouns.)
(i) *Her book* is here. *Your book* is over there.	Possessive adjectives are followed immediately by a noun; they do not stand alone.
(j) A bird uses *its* wings to fly. (k) *INCORRECT:* A bird uses *it's* wings to fly. (l) *It's* cold today. (m) The Harbour Inn is my favorite old hotel. *It's been* in business since 1933.	COMPARE: *Its* has NO APOSTROPHE when it is used as a possessive, as in (j). *It's* has an apostrophe when it is used as a contraction of *it is,* as in (l), or *it has* when *has* is part of the present perfect tense, as in (m).

8-2 PERSONAL PRONOUNS: AGREEMENT WITH GENERIC NOUNS AND INDEFINITE PRONOUNS

(a) *A student* walked into the room. *She* was looking for the teacher. (b) *A student* walked into the room. *He* was looking for the teacher.	In (a) and (b): The pronouns refer to particular individuals whose gender is known. The nouns are not generic.
(c) *A student* should always do *his* assignments. (d) *A student* should always do *his/her* assignments. *A student* should always do *his or her* assignments.	A generic noun* does not refer to any person or thing in particular; rather, it represents a whole group. In (c): *A student* is a generic noun; it refers to *anyone who is a student*. With a generic noun, a singular masculine pronoun has been used traditionally, but many English speakers now use both masculine and feminine pronouns to refer to a singular generic noun, as in (d). The use of both masculine and feminine pronouns can create awkward-sounding sentences.
(e) *Students* should always do *their* assignments.	Problems with choosing masculine and/or feminine pronouns can often be avoided by using a plural rather than a singular generic noun, as in (e).

INDEFINITE PRONOUNS			
everyone	*someone*	*anyone*	*no one***
everybody	*somebody*	*anybody*	*nobody*
everything	*something*	*anything*	*nothing*

(f) *Somebody* left *his* book on the desk. (g) *Everyone* has *his or her* own ideas. (h) INFORMAL: *Somebody* left *their* book on the desk. *Everyone* has *their* own ideas.	A singular pronoun is used in formal English to refer to an indefinite pronoun, as in (f) and (g). In everyday informal English, a plural personal pronoun is often used to refer to an indefinite pronoun, as in (h).

*See Chart 7-7, p. 34, *Basic Article Usage*.

***No one* can also be written with a hyphen in British English: *No-one* heard me.

8-3 PERSONAL PRONOUNS: AGREEMENT WITH COLLECTIVE NOUNS

EXAMPLES OF COLLECTIVE NOUNS			
audience	*couple*	*family*	*public*
class	*crowd*	*government*	*staff*
committee	*faculty*	*group*	*team*

(a) *My family* is large. *It* is composed of nine members.	When a collective noun refers to a single impersonal unit, a singular gender-neutral pronoun (*it, its*) is used, as in (a).
(b) *My family* is loving and supportive. *They* are always ready to help me.	When a collective noun refers to a collection of various individuals, a plural pronoun (*they, them, their*) is used, as in (b).*

*NOTE: When the collective noun refers to a collection of individuals, the verb may be either singular or plural: *My family is* OR *are loving and supportive.* A singular verb is generally preferred in American English. A plural verb is used more frequently in British English, especially with the words *government* or *public*. (American: *The government is* planning many changes. British: *The government are* planning many changes.)

8-4 REFLEXIVE PRONOUNS

SINGULAR	PLURAL
myself	*ourselves*
yourself	*yourselves*
herself, himself, itself, oneself	*themselves*

(a) Larry was in the theater. I *saw him*. I talked *to him*.	Compare (a) and (b): Usually an object pronoun is used as the object of a verb or preposition, as **him** in (a). (See Chart 8-1, p. 38.)
(b) *I saw myself* in the mirror. *I looked at myself* for a long time.	A *reflexive pronoun* is used as the object of a verb or preposition when the subject of the sentence and the object are the same person, as in (b).★ *I* and *myself* are the same person.
(c) *INCORRECT:* I saw *me* in the mirror.	
—Did someone fax the report to Mr. Lee? —Yes. —Are you sure? (d) —Yes. *I myself* faxed the report to him. (e) —*I* faxed the report to him *myself*.	Reflexive pronouns are also used for emphasis. In (d): The speaker would say "I myself" strongly, with emphasis. The emphatic reflexive pronoun can immediately follow a noun or pronoun, as in (d), or come at the end of the clause, as in (e).
(f) Anna lives *by herself*.	The expression *by* + *a reflexive pronoun* means "alone."

★Sometimes, but relatively infrequently, an object pronoun is used as the object of a preposition even when the subject and object pronoun are the same person. Examples: *I* took my books with **me**. **Bob** brought his books with **him**. *I* looked around **me**. **She** kept her son close to **her**.

Anna drew a picture of **herself**.
All of the students drew pictures of **themselves**.

8-5 USING *YOU*, *ONE*, AND *THEY* AS IMPERSONAL PRONOUNS

(a) *One* should always be polite. (b) How does *one* get to 5th Avenue from here? (c) *You* should always be polite. (d) How do *you* get to 5th Avenue from here?	In (a) and (b): *One* means "any person, people in general." In (c) and (d): *You* means "any person, people in general." *One* is much more formal than *you*. Impersonal *you,* rather than *one,* is used more frequently in everyday English.
(e) *One* should take care of *one's* health. (f) *One* should take care of *his* health. (g) *One* should take care of *his or her* health.	Notice the pronouns that may be used in the same sentence to refer back to *one:* (e) is typical in British usage and formal American usage. (f) is principally American usage. (g) is stylistically awkward.

(h) — Did Ann lose her job?
    — Yes. *They* fired her.
 (i) — *They* mine graphite in Brazil, don't they?
    — Yes. Brazil is one of the leading graphite producers in the world.
	They is used as an impersonal pronoun in spoken or very informal English to mean "some people or somebody."*
	 They has no stated antecedent. The antecedent is implied. In (h): *They* = the people Ann worked for.

*In written or more formal English, the passive is generally preferred to the use of impersonal *they:*
   Active: *They fired her.*   Active: *They mine graphite in Brazil, don't they?*
   Passive: *She was fired.*   Passive: *Graphite is mined in Brazil, isn't it?*

8-6 FORMS OF *OTHER*

	ADJECTIVE	PRONOUN	
SINGULAR PLURAL	*another* book (is) *other* books (are)	*another* (is) *others* (are)	Forms of *other* are used as either adjectives or pronouns. Notice: A final *-s* is used only for a plural pronoun *(others)*.
SINGULAR PLURAL	*the other* book (is) *the other* books (are)	*the other* (is) *the others* (are)	

(a) The students in the class come from many countries. One of the students is from Mexico. *Another student is* from Iraq. *Another is* from Japan. *Other students are* from Brazil. *Others are* from Algeria.	The meaning of *another: one more in addition to the one(s) already mentioned.* The meaning of *other* / *others* (without *the*): *several more in addition to the one(s) already mentioned.*
(b) I have three books. Two are mine. *The other book* is yours. *(The other is yours.)* (c) I have three books. One is mine. *The other books* are yours. *(The others are yours.)*	The meaning of *the other(s): all that remains from a given number; the rest of a specific group.*
(d) I will be here for *another three years*. (e) I need *another five dollars*. (f) We drove *another ten miles*.	*Another* is used as an adjective with expressions of time, money, and distance, even if these expressions contain plural nouns. *Another* means "an additional" in these expressions.

(a) We write to *each other* every week. We write to *one another* every week.	***Each other*** and ***one another*** indicate a reciprocal relationship.* In (a): I write to him every week, and he writes to me every week.

(b) Please write on *every other* line.
I see her *every other* week.
	Every other can give the idea of "alternate." In (b):
	    Write on the first line.
	    Do not write on the second line.
	    Write on the third line.
	    Do not write on the fourth line.
	    (Etc.)

(c) —Have you seen Ali recently? —Yes. I saw him just *the other day*.	***The other*** is used in time expressions such as *the other day, the other morning, the other week, etc.*, to refer to the recent past. In (c): ***the other day*** means "a few days ago, not long ago."
(d) The ducklings walked in a line behind the mother duck. Then the mother duck slipped into the pond. The ducklings followed her. They slipped into the water *one after the other*. (e) They slipped into the water *one after another*.	In (d): ***one after the other*** expresses the idea that separate actions occur very close in time. In (e): ***one after another*** has the same meaning as ***one after the other***.

(f) No one knows my secret *other than* Rosa. (g) No one knows my secret *except (for)* Rosa.	In (f): ***other than*** is usually used after a negative to mean "except." (g) has the same meaning.
(h) Fruit and vegetables are full of vitamins and minerals. ***In other words***, they are good for you.	In (h): ***In other words*** is used to explain, usually in simpler or clearer terms, the meaning of the preceding sentence(s).

*In typical usage, *each other* and *one another* are interchangeable; there is no difference between them. Some native speakers, however, use *each other* when they are talking about only two persons or things, and *one another* when there are more than two.

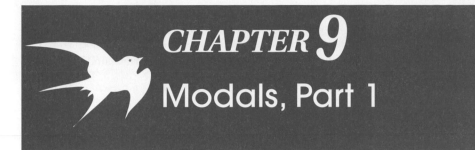

CHAPTER 9
Modals, Part 1

9-1 INTRODUCTION

The modal auxiliaries in English are **can, could, had better, may, might, must, ought (to), shall, should, will, would**.

Modal auxiliaries generally express speakers' attitudes. For example, modals can express that a speaker feels something is necessary, advisable, permissible, possible, or probable; and, in addition, they can convey the strength of those attitudes.

Each modal has more than one meaning or use. See Chart 10-10, p. 54, for a summary overview of modals.

(a) BASIC MODALS
 	
I
You
He
She
It **} +** { ***can*** *do* it.
We   ***could*** *do* it.
You   ***had better*** *do* it.
They   ***may*** *do* it.
          might *do* it.
          must *do* it.
          ought to *do* it.
          shall *do* it.
          should *do* it.
          will *do* it.
          would *do* it.
	Modals do not take a final **-s**, even when the subject is *she, he,* or *it*.
	    SMALL CORRECT: ***She can*** do it.
	    INCORRECT: She *cans* do it.

	Modals are followed immediately by the simple form of a verb.
	    CORRECT: ***She can do*** it.
	    INCORRECT: She can *to* do it. / She can *does* it. / She can *did* it.
	
	The only exception is **ought,** which is followed by an infinitive (***to*** + *the simple form of a verb*).
	    CORRECT: He ***ought to go*** to the meeting.

(b) PHRASAL MODALS **be able to** *do* it **be going to** *do* it **be supposed to** *do* it **have to** *do* it **have got to** *do* it **used to** *do* it	Phrasal modals are common expressions whose meanings are similar to those of some of the modal auxiliaries. For example: **be able to** is similar to **can; be going to** is similar to **will**. An infinitive (***to*** + *the simple form of a verb*) is used in these similar expressions.

9-2 POLITE REQUESTS WITH *"I"* AS THE SUBJECT

MAY I COULD I	(a) *May I* (please) *borrow* your pen? (b) *Could I borrow* your pen (please)?	*May I* and *could I* are used to request permission. They are equally polite.★ Note in (b): In a polite request, *could* has a present or future meaning, not a past meaning.
CAN I	(c) *Can I borrow* your pen?	*Can I* is used informally to request permission, especially if the speaker is talking to someone s/he knows fairly well. *Can I* is usually considered a little less polite than *may I* or *could I*.
	TYPICAL RESPONSES Certainly. Yes, certainly. Of course. Yes, of course. Sure. *(informal)*	Often the response to a polite request is an action, such as a nod or shake of the head, or a simple "uh-huh."

★*Might* is also possible: *Might I borrow* your pen? *Might I* is quite formal and polite; it is used much less frequently than *may I* or *could I*.

9-3 POLITE REQUESTS WITH *"YOU"* AS THE SUBJECT

WOULD YOU WILL YOU	(a) *Would you pass* the salt (please)? (b) *Will you* (please) *pass* the salt?	The meaning of *would you* and *will you* in a polite request is the same. *Would you* is more common and is often considered more polite. The degree of politeness, however, is often determined by the speaker's tone of voice.
COULD YOU	(c) *Could you pass* the salt (please)?	Basically, *could you* and *would you* have the same meaning. The difference is slight: *Would you* = *Do you want to do this please?* *Could you* = *Do you want to do this please, and is it possible for you to do this?* *Could you* and *would you* are equally polite.
CAN YOU	(d) *Can you* (please) *pass* the salt?	*Can you* is often used informally. It usually sounds less polite than *could you* or *would you*.
	TYPICAL RESPONSES Yes, I'd (I would) be happy to/be glad to. Certainly. Sure. *(informal)*	A person usually responds in the affirmative to a polite request. If a negative response is necessary, a person might begin by saying "I'd like to, but . . . " (e.g., "I'd like to pass the salt, but I can't reach it").
	(e) *INCORRECT: May you* pass the salt?	*May* is used only with *I* or *we* in polite requests.

9-4 POLITE REQUESTS WITH *WOULD YOU MIND*

ASKING PERMISSION (a) *Would you mind if I closed* the window? (b) *Would you mind if I used* the phone?	Notice in (a): ***Would you mind if I*** is followed by the simple past.★ The meaning in (a): *May I close the window? Is it all right if I close the window? Will it cause you any trouble or discomfort if I close the window?*
TYPICAL RESPONSES No, not at all/of course not. No, that would be fine.	Another typical response might be "unh-unh," meaning "no."
ASKING SOMEONE TO DO SOMETHING (c) *Would you mind **closing** the window?* (d) Excuse me. *Would you mind **repeating** that?*	Notice in (c): ***Would you mind*** is followed by ***-ing*** (a gerund). The meaning in (c): *I don't want to cause you any trouble, but would you please close the window? Would that cause you any inconvenience?*
TYPICAL RESPONSES No. I'd be happy to. Not at all. I'd be glad to. Sure./Okay. *(informal)*	The informal responses of "Sure" and "Okay" are common, but are not logical: the speaker means "No, I wouldn't mind" but seems to be saying "Yes, I would mind." Native speakers understand that the response "Sure" or "Okay" in this situation means that the speaker agrees to the request.

*Sometimes, in informal spoken English, the simple present is used: *Would you mind if I **close** the window?*
(NOTE: The simple past does not refer to past time after ***would you mind;*** it refers to present or future time. See Chart 20-3, p. 101, for more information.)

9-5 EXPRESSING NECESSITY: *MUST, HAVE TO, HAVE GOT TO*

(a) All applicants *must take* an entrance exam. (b) All applicants *have to take* an entrance exam.	***Must*** and ***have to*** both express necessity. In (a) and (b): It is necessary for every applicant to take an entrance exam. There is no other choice. The exam is required.
(c) I'm looking for Sue. I *have to talk* to her about our lunch date tomorrow. I can't meet her for lunch because I *have to go* to a business meeting at 1:00. (d) Where's Sue? I *must talk* to her right away. I have an urgent message for her.	In everyday statements of necessity, ***have to*** is used more commonly than ***must***. ***Must*** is usually stronger than ***have to*** and can indicate urgency or stress importance. In (c): The speaker is simply saying, "I need to do this, and I need to do that." In (d): The speaker is strongly saying, "This is very important!"
(e) I *have to* ("hafta") be home by eight. (f) He *has to* ("hasta") go to a meeting tonight.	Note: ***have to*** is usually pronounced "hafta"; ***has to*** is usually pronounced "hasta."
(g) I *have got to go* now. I have a class in ten minutes. (h) I *have to go* now. I have a class in ten minutes.	***Have got to*** also expresses the idea of necessity: (g) and (h) have the same meaning. ***Have got to*** is informal and is used primarily in spoken English. ***Have to*** is used in both formal and informal English.
(i) I *have got to go* ("I've gotta go/I gotta go") now.	Usual pronunciation of ***got to*** is "gotta." Sometimes ***have*** is dropped in speech: "I gotta do it."

(j) PRESENT OR FUTURE
 	
   I *have to* / *have got to* / *must study* tonight.
(k) PAST
 	
   I *had to study* last night.
	The idea of past necessity is expressed by ***had to***. There is no other past form for ***must*** (when it means necessity) or ***have got to***.

9-6 LACK OF NECESSITY AND PROHIBITION: *HAVE TO* AND *MUST* IN THE NEGATIVE

LACK OF NECESSITY (a) Tomorrow is a holiday. We *don't have to go* to class. (b) I can hear you. You *don't have to shout.*★	When used in the negative, *must* and *have to* have different meanings.
	do not have to = lack of necessity In (a): It is not necessary for us to go to class tomorrow because it is a holiday.
PROHIBITION (c) You *must not look* in the closet. Your birthday present is hidden there. (d) You *must not tell* anyone my secret. Do you promise?	*must not* = prohibition (DO NOT DO THIS!) In (c): Do not look in the closet. I forbid it. Looking in the closet is prohibited. Negative contraction: *mustn't*. (The first "t" is silent: "muss-ənt.")

★Lack of necessity may also be expressed by *need not* + *the simple form of a verb*: You *needn't shout*. The use of *needn't* as an auxiliary is chiefly British except in certain common expressions such as "You needn't worry."

9-7 ADVISABILITY: *SHOULD, OUGHT TO, HAD BETTER*

(a) You *should study* harder. You *ought to study* harder. (b) Drivers *should obey* the speed limit. Drivers *ought to obey* the speed limit.	*Should* and *ought to* have the same meaning: they express advisability. The meaning ranges in strength from a suggestion ("This is a good idea") to a statement about responsibility or duty ("This is a very important thing to do"). In (a): "This is a good idea. This is my advice." In (b): "This is an important responsibility."
(c) You *shouldn't leave* your keys in the car.	Negative contraction: *shouldn't*.★
(d) I *ought to* ("otta") *study* tonight, but I think I'll watch TV instead.	*Ought to* is often pronounced "otta" in informal speaking.
(e) The gas tank is almost empty. We *had better stop* at the next service station. (f) You *had better take* care of that cut on your hand soon, or it will get infected.	In meaning, *had better* is close to *should/ought to*, but *had better* is usually stronger. Often *had better* implies a warning or a threat of possible bad consequences. In (e): If we don't stop at a service station, there will be a bad result. We will run out of gas. Notes on the use of *had better:* • It has a present or future meaning. • It is followed by the simple form of a verb. • It is more common in speaking than writing.
(g) You*'d better* take care of it. (h) You *better* take care of it.	Contraction: *'d better,* as in (g). Sometimes in speaking, *had* is dropped, as in (h).
(i) You*'d better not* be late.	Negative form: *had better* + *not*.

★*Ought to* is not commonly used in the negative. If it is used in the negative, the *to* is sometimes dropped: *You oughtn't (to) leave your keys in the car.*

9-8 THE PAST FORM OF *SHOULD*

(a) I had a test this morning. I didn't do well on the test because I didn't study for it last night. I **should have studied** last night.	Past form: **should have** + *past participle.*★
(b) You were supposed to be here at 10 P.M., but you didn't come until midnight. We were worried about you. You **should have called** us. (You did not call.)	In (a): *I should have studied* means that studying was a good idea, but I didn't do it. I made a mistake.
	Usual pronunciation of **should have:** "should-əv" or "should-ə."
(c) My back hurts. I **should not have carried** that heavy box up two flights of stairs. (I carried the box, and now I'm sorry.)	In (c): *I should not have carried* means that I carried something, but it turned out to be a bad idea. I made a mistake.
(d) We went to a movie, but it was a waste of time and money. We **should not have gone** to the movie.	Usual pronunciation of **should not have:** "shouldn't-əv" or "shouldn't-ə."

★The past form of **ought to** is **ought to have** + *past participle. (I ought to have studied.)* It has the same meaning as the past form of **should**. In the past, **should** is used more commonly than **ought to**. **Had better** is used only rarely in a past form (e.g., He **had better have taken care of it**) and usually only in speaking, not writing.

9-9 EXPECTATIONS: *BE SUPPOSED TO*

(a) The game **is supposed to begin** at 10:00.	**Be supposed to** expresses the idea that someone (I, we, they, the teacher, lots of people, my father, etc.) expects something to happen. **Be supposed to** often expresses expectations about scheduled events, as in (a), or correct procedures, as in (b).
(b) The committee **is supposed to vote** by secret ballot.	
(c) I **am supposed to go** to the meeting. My boss told me that he wants me to attend.	**Be supposed to** also expresses expectations about behavior.
(d) The children **are supposed to put away** their toys before they go to bed.	In (c) and (d): **be supposed to** gives the idea that someone else expects (requests or requires) certain behavior.
(e) Jack **was supposed to call** me last night. I wonder why he didn't.	**Be supposed to** in the past *(was/were supposed to)* expresses unfulfilled expectations. In (e): The speaker expected Jack to call, but he didn't.

9-10 MAKING SUGGESTIONS: *LET'S, WHY DON'T, SHALL I/WE*

(a) *Let's go* to a movie. (b) *Let's not go* to a movie. 　*Let's stay* home instead.	*Let's = let us*. *Let's* is followed by the simple form of a verb. Negative form: *let's + not + simple verb* The meaning of *let's*: "I have a suggestion for us."
(c) *Why don't we go* to a movie? (d) *Why don't you come* around seven? (e) *Why don't I give* Mary a call?	*Why don't* is used primarily in spoken English to make a friendly suggestion. In (c): *Why don't we go* = *let's go.* In (d): I suggest that you come around seven. In (e): Should I give Mary a call? Do you agree with my suggestion?
(f) *Shall I open* the window? Is that okay with you? (g) *Shall we leave* at two? Is that okay? (h) Let's go, *shall we?* (i) Let's go, *okay?*	When *shall* is used with *I* or *we* in a question, the speaker is usually making a suggestion and asking another person if s/he agrees with this suggestion. This use of *shall* is relatively formal and infrequent. Sometimes "shall we?" is used as a tag question after *let's*, as in (h). More informally, "okay?" is used as a tag question, as in (i).

9-11 MAKING SUGGESTIONS: *COULD* vs. *SHOULD*

—*What should we do tomorrow?* (a) Why don't we go on a picnic? (b) We *could go* on a picnic.	*Could* can be used to make suggestions. (a) and (b) are similar in meaning: the speaker is suggesting a picnic.
—*I'm having trouble in math class.* (c) You *should talk* to your teacher. (d) *Maybe* you *should talk* to your teacher. —*I'm having trouble in math class.* (e) You *could talk* to your teacher. Or you *could ask* Ann to help you with your math lessons. Or I *could try* to help you.	*Should* gives definite advice. In (c), the speaker is saying: "I believe it is important for you to do this. This is what I recommend." In (d), the use of *maybe* softens the strength of the advice. *Could* offers suggestions or possibilities. In (e), the speaker is saying: "I have some possible suggestions for you. It is possible to do this. Or it is possible to do that."*
—*I failed my math class.* (f) You *should have talked* to your teacher and gotten some help from her during the term. —*I failed my math class.* (g) You *could have talked* to your teacher. Or you *could have asked* Ann to help you with your math. Or I *could have tried* to help you.	*Should have* gives "hindsight advice."** In (f), the speaker is saying: "It was important for you to talk to the teacher, but you didn't do it. You made a mistake." *Could have* offers "hindsight possibilities."** In (g), the speaker is saying: "You had the chance to do this or that. It was possible for this or that to happen. You missed some good opportunities."

*Might (but not *may*) can also be used to make suggestions (*You might talk to your teacher*), but the use of *could* is more common.

**"Hindsight" refers to looking at something after it happens.

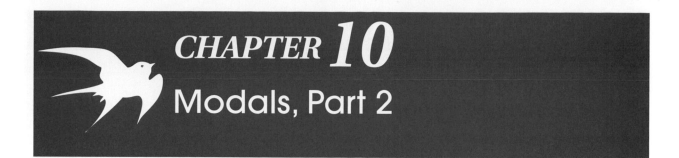

CHAPTER 10
Modals, Part 2

10-1 DEGREES OF CERTAINTY: PRESENT TIME

—*Why isn't John in class?* **100% sure**: He ***is*** sick. **95% sure**: He ***must be*** sick. **less than 50% sure**: { He ***may be*** sick. He ***might be*** sick. He ***could be*** sick.	"Degree of certainty" refers to how sure we are—what we think the chances are—that something is true. If we are sure something is true in the present, we don't need to use a modal. For example, if I say, "John is sick," I am sure; I am stating a fact that I am sure is true. My degree of certainty is 100%.
—*Why isn't John in class?* (a) He ***must be*** sick. (Usually he is in class every day, but when I saw him last night, he wasn't feeling good. So my best guess is that he is sick today. I can't think of another possibility.)	***Must*** expresses a strong degree of certainty about a present situation, but the degree of certainty is still less than 100%.
	In (a): The speaker is saying, "Probably John is sick. I have evidence to make me believe that he is sick. That is my logical conclusion, but I do not know for certain."
—*Why isn't John in class?* (b) He ***may be*** sick. (c) He ***might be*** sick. (d) He ***could be*** sick. (I don't really know. He may be at home watching TV. He might be at the library. He could be out of town.)	***May, might,*** and ***could*** express a weak degree of certainty.
	In (b), (c), and (d): The speaker is saying, "Perhaps, maybe,* possibly John is sick. I am only making a guess. I can think of other possibilities." (b), (c), and (d) have the same meaning.

*__*Maybe*__ (one word) is an adverb: __*Maybe*__ *he is sick.*
  __*May be*__ (two words) is a verb form: *He __may be__ sick.*

Harry is coughing and sneezing, blowing
his nose, and running a fever.
He ***must have*** the flu.

10-2 DEGREES OF CERTAINTY: PRESENT TIME NEGATIVE

100% sure:	Sam *isn't* hungry.	
99% sure:	{	Sam *couldn't be* hungry. Sam *can't be* hungry.
95% sure:	Sam *must not be* hungry.	
less than 50% sure:	{	Sam *may not be* hungry. Sam *might not be* hungry.

(a) Sam doesn't want anything to eat. He *isn't* hungry. He told me his stomach is full. I heard him say that he isn't hungry. I believe him.	In (a): The speaker is sure that Sam is not hungry.
(b) Sam *couldn't/can't be* hungry! That's impossible! I just saw him eat a huge meal. He has already eaten enough to fill two grown men. Did he really say he'd like something to eat? I don't believe it.	In (b): The speaker believes that there is no possibility that Sam is hungry (but the speaker is not 100% sure). When used in the negative to show degree of certainty, *couldn't* and *can't* forcefully express the idea that the speaker believes something is impossible.
(c) Sam isn't eating his food. He *must not be* hungry. That's the only reason I can think of.	In (c): The speaker is expressing a logical conclusion, a "best guess."
(d) I don't know why Sam isn't eating his food. He *may not/might not be* hungry right now. Or maybe he doesn't feel well. Or perhaps he ate just before he got here. Who knows?	In (d): The speaker uses *may not/might not* to mention a possibility.

10-3 DEGREES OF CERTAINTY: PAST TIME

PAST TIME: AFFIRMATIVE
 	
—*Why wasn't Mary in class?*
(a)   **100%**:   She *was* sick.
 	
(b)   **95%**:   She *must have been* sick.
 	
(c) **less than 50%**: { She *may have been* sick.
                   She *might have been* sick.
                   She *could have been* sick.
	In (a): The speaker is sure.
	
	In (b): The speaker is making a logical conclusion, e.g., "I saw Mary yesterday and found out that she was sick. I assume that is the reason why she was absent. I can't think of any other good reason."
	
	In (c): The speaker is mentioning one possibility.

PAST TIME: NEGATIVE
 	
—*Why didn't Sam eat?*
(d)   **100%**:   Sam *wasn't* hungry.
 	
(e)   **99%**: { Sam *couldn't have been* hungry.
              Sam *can't have been* hungry.
 	
(f)   **95%**:   Sam *must not have* been hungry.
 	
(g) **less than 50%**: { Sam *may not have been* hungry.
                Sam *might not have been* hungry.
	In (d): The speaker is sure.
	
	In (e): The speaker believes that it is impossible for Sam to have been hungry.
	
	In (f): The speaker is making a logical conclusion.
	
	In (g): The speaker is mentioning one possibility.

10-4 DEGREES OF CERTAINTY: FUTURE TIME

100% sure:	Kay *will do* well on the test.	→ The speaker feels sure.
90% sure: {	Kay *should do* well on the test. Kay *ought to do* well on the test. }	→ The speaker is almost sure.
less than 50% sure: {	She *may do* well on the test. She *might do* well on the test. She *could do* well on the test. }	→ The speaker is guessing.

(a) Kay has been studying hard. She *should do* / *ought to do* well on the test tomorrow.	*Should* / *ought to* can be used to express expectations about future events. In (a): The speaker is saying, "Kay will probably do well on the test. I expect her to do well. That is what I think will happen."
(b) I wonder why Sue hasn't written us. We *should have heard* / *ought to have heard* from her last week.	The past form of *should* / *ought to* is used to mean that the speaker expected something that did not occur.

10-5 PROGRESSIVE FORMS OF MODALS

(a) Let's just knock on the door lightly. Tom *may be sleeping.* *(right now)* (b) All of the lights in Ann's room are turned off. She *must be sleeping.* *(right now)*	Progressive form, present time: *modal* + *be* + *-ing* Meaning: *in progress right now*
(c) Sue wasn't at home last night when we went to visit her. She *might have been studying* at the library. (d) Joe wasn't at home last night. He has a lot of exams coming up soon, and he is also working on a term paper. He *must have been studying* at the library.	Progressive form, past time: *modal* + *have been* + *-ing* Meaning: *in progress at a time in the past*

10-6 ABILITY: *CAN* AND *COULD*

(a) Tom is strong. He *can lift* that heavy box. (b) I *can see* Central Park from my apartment.	***Can*** is used to express physical ability, as in (a). ***Can*** is frequently used with verbs of the five senses: *see, hear, feel, smell, taste,* as in (b).
(c) Maria *can play* the piano. She's been taking lessons for many years.	***Can*** is used to express an acquired skill. In (c), *can play = knows how to play.*
(d) You *can buy* a hammer at the hardware store.	***Can*** is used to express possibility. In (d), *you can buy = it is possible for one to buy.*
COMPARE (e) I'm not quite ready to go, but you *can leave* if you're in a hurry. I'll meet you later. (f) When you finish the test, you *may leave*.	***Can*** is used to give permission in informal situations, as in (e). In formal situations, ***may*** rather than ***can*** is usually used to give permission, as in (f).
(g) Dogs *can bark*, but they *cannot / can't talk*.	Negative form: ***cannot*** or ***can't***.
(h) Tom *could lift* the box, but I *couldn't*.	The past form of ***can*** meaning "ability" is ***could***, as in (h). Negative = ***could not*** or ***couldn't***.

10-7 USING *WOULD* TO EXPRESS A REPEATED ACTION IN THE PAST

(a) When I was a child, my father *would read* me a story at night before bedtime. (b) When I was a child, my father *used to read* me a story at night before bedtime.	***Would*** can be used to express an *action* that was repeated regularly in the past. When ***would*** is used to express this idea, it has the same meaning as ***used to*** *(habitual past)*. (a) and (b) have the same meaning.
(c) I *used to live* in California. He *used to be* a Boy Scout. They *used to have* a Ford.	***Used to*** expresses an habitual situation that existed in the past, as in (c). In this case, ***would*** may not be used as an alternative. ***Would*** is used only for regularly repeated actions in the past.

When I was a child, I **would take** a flashlight
to bed with me so that I could read comic books
without my parents' knowing about it.

10-8 EXPRESSING PREFERENCE: *WOULD RATHER*

(a) I *would rather go* to a movie tonight *than study* grammar. (b) I'*d rather study* history than *(study)* biology.	***Would rather*** expresses preference. In (a): Notice that the simple form of a verb follows both ***would rather*** and ***than***. In (b): If the verb is the same, it usually is not repeated after ***than***.
—How much do you weigh? (c) I'*d rather not tell* you.	Contraction: ***I would*** = ***I'd*** Negative form: ***would rather*** + ***not***
(d) The movie was okay, but I *would rather have gone* to the concert last night.	The past form: ***would rather have*** + *past participle* Usual pronunciation: "I'd rather-əv"
(e) I'*d rather be lying* on a beach in India than *(be)* sitting in class right now.	Progressive form: ***would rather*** + ***be*** + ***-ing***

10-9 COMBINING MODALS WITH PHRASAL MODALS

(a) *INCORRECT:* Janet *will can* help you tomorrow.	A modal cannot be immediately followed by another modal. In (a): The modal ***will*** cannot be followed by ***can***, which is another modal.
(b) CORRECT: Janet *will be able to* help you tomorrow.	A modal can, however, be followed by the phrasal modals ***be able to*** and ***have to***. In (b): The modal ***will*** is correctly followed by the phrasal modal ***be able to***.
(c) CORRECT: Tom *isn't going to be able to* help you tomorrow.	It is also sometimes possible for one phrasal modal to follow another phrasal modal. In (c): ***be going to*** is followed by ***be able to***.

10-10 SUMMARY CHART OF MODALS AND SIMILAR EXPRESSIONS

AUXILIARY	USES	PRESENT/FUTURE	PAST
may	(1) polite request *(only with I or we)*	*May* I *borrow* your pen?	
	(2) formal permission	You *may leave* the room.	
	(3) less than 50% certainty	—*Where's John?* He *may be* at the library.	He *may have been* at the library.
might	(1) less than 50% certainty	—*Where's John?* He *might be* at the library.	He *might have been* at the library.
	(2) polite request *(rare)*	*Might* I *borrow* your pen?	
should	(1) advisability	I *should study* tonight.	I *should have studied* last night, but I didn't.
	(2) 90% certainty *(expectation)*	She *should do* well on the test. *(future only, not present)*	She *should have done* well on the test.
ought to	(1) advisability	I *ought to study* tonight.	I *ought to have studied* last night, but I didn't.
	(2) 90% certainty *(expectation)*	She *ought to do* well on the test. *(future only, not present)*	She *ought to have done* well on the test.
had better	(1) advisability with threat of bad result	You *had better be* on time, or we will leave without you.	*(past form uncommon)*
be supposed to	(1) expectation	Class *is supposed to begin* at 10:00.	
	(2) unfulfilled expectation		Class *was supposed to begin* at 10:00, but it didn't begin until 10:15.
must	(1) strong necessity	I *must go* to class today.	(I *had to go* to class yesterday.)
	(2) prohibition *(negative)*	You *must not* open that door.	
	(3) 95% certainty	Mary isn't in class. She *must be* sick. *(present only)*	Mary *must have been* sick yesterday.
have to	(1) necessity	I *have to go* to class today.	I *had to go* to class yesterday.
	(2) lack of necessity *(negative)*	I *don't have to go* to class today.	I *didn't have to go* to class yesterday.
have got to	(1) necessity	I *have got to go* to class today.	(I *had to go* to class yesterday.)
will	(1) 100% certainty	He *will be* here at 6:00. *(future only)*	
	(2) willingness	—*The phone's ringing.* I*'ll get* it.	
	(3) polite request	*Will* you please *pass* the salt?	

AUXILIARY	USES	PRESENT/FUTURE	PAST
be going to	(1) 100% certainty *(prediction)*	He *is going to be* here at 6:00. *(future only)*	
	(2) definite plan *(intention)*	I*'m going to paint* my bedroom. *(future only)*	
	(3) unfulfilled intention		I *was going to paint* my room, but I didn't have time.
can	(1) ability/possibility	I *can run* fast.	I *could run* fast when I was a child, but now I can't.
	(2) informal permission	You *can use* my car tomorrow.	
	(3) informal polite request	*Can* I *borrow* your pen?	
	(4) impossibility *(negative only)*	That *can't be* true!	That *can't have been* true!
could	(1) past ability		I *could run* fast when I was a child.
	(2) polite request	*Could* I *borrow* your pen? *Could* you *help* me?	
	(3) suggestion *(affirmative only)*	—I need help in math. You *could talk* to your teacher.	You *could have talked* to your teacher.
	(4) less than 50% certainty	—Where's John? He *could be* at home.	He *could have been* at home.
	(5) impossibility *(negative only)*	That *couldn't be* true!	That *couldn't have been* true!
be able to	(1) ability	I *am able to help* you. I *will be able to help* you.	I *was able to help* him.
would	(1) polite request	*Would* you please *pass* the salt? *Would* you *mind* if I left early?	
	(2) preference	I *would rather go* to the park than *stay* home.	I *would rather have gone* to the park.
	(3) repeated action in the past		When I was a child, I *would visit* my grandparents every weekend.
	(4) polite for "want" *(with* like*)*	I *would like* an apple, please.	
	(5) unfulfilled wish		I *would have liked* a cookie, but there were none in the house.
used to	(1) repeated action in the past		I *used to visit* my grandparents every weekend.
	(2) past situation that no longer exists		I *used to live* in Spain. Now I live in Korea.
shall	(1) polite question to make a suggestion	*Shall* I *open* the window?	
	(2) future with "I" or "we" as subject	I *shall arrive* at nine. *(will = more common)*	

NOTE: Use of modals in reported speech is discussed in Chart 12-7, p. 65. Use of modals in conditional sentences is discussed in Chapter 20.

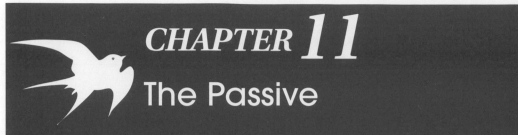

CHAPTER 11
The Passive

FORMING THE PASSIVE

ACTIVE: (a) subject verb object Mary *helped* the boy.	In the passive, *the object* of an active verb becomes *the subject* of the passive verb: ***the boy*** in (a) becomes the subject of the passive verb in (b). Notice that the subject of an active verb follows ***by*** in a passive sentence. The noun that follows ***by*** is called the "agent." In (b): ***Mary*** is the agent. (a) and (b) have the same meaning.
PASSIVE: (b) subject verb The boy *was helped* by Mary.	
ACTIVE: (c) An accident *happened*. PASSIVE: (d) (none)	Only transitive verbs (verbs that can be followed by an object) are used in the passive. It is not possible to use intransitive verbs (such as *happen, sleep, come, seem*) in the passive. (See Appendix Chart A-1, p. A1.)

Form of the passive: ***be*** + *past participle*

	ACTIVE				PASSIVE		
simple present	Mary	*helps*	the boy.	The boy	*is*	*helped*	by Mary.
present progressive	Mary	*is helping*	the boy.	The boy	*is being*	*helped*	by Mary.
*present perfect**	Mary	*has helped*	the boy.	The boy	*has been*	*helped*	by Mary.
simple past	Mary	*helped*	the boy.	The boy	*was*	*helped*	by Mary.
past progressive	Mary	*was helping*	the boy.	The boy	*was being*	*helped*	by Mary.
*past perfect**	Mary	*had helped*	the boy.	The boy	*had been*	*helped*	by Mary.
*simple future**	Mary	*will help*	the boy.	The boy	*will be*	*helped*	by Mary.
be going to	Mary	*is going to help*	the boy.	The boy	*is going to be*	*helped*	by Mary.
*future perfect**	Mary	*will have helped*	the boy.	The boy	*will have been*	*helped*	by Mary.

(e) ***Was* the boy** *helped* by Mary? (f) ***Is* the boy** *being helped* by Mary? (g) ***Has* the boy** *been helped* by Mary?	In the question form of passive verbs, an auxiliary verb precedes the subject. (See Appendix Chart B-1, p. A5, for information about question forms.)

*The progressive forms of the *present perfect, past perfect, future,* and *future perfect* are very rarely used in the passive.

11-2 USING THE PASSIVE

(a) Rice *is grown* in India. (b) Our house *was built* in 1980. (c) This olive oil *was imported* from Crete.	Usually the passive is used without a *by*-phrase. The passive is most frequently used when it is not known or not important to know exactly who performs an action. In (a): Rice is grown in India by people, by farmers, by someone. It is not known or important to know exactly who grows rice in India. (a), (b), and (c) illustrate the most common use of the passive, i.e., without the *by*-phrase.
(d) *Life on the Mississippi was written* by Mark Twain.	The *by*-phrase is included only if it is important to know who performs an action, as in (d), where *by Mark Twain* is important information.
(e) My aunt *made* this rug. *(active)*	If the speaker knows who performs an action, usually the active is used, as in (e).
(f) This rug *was made* by my aunt. That rug *was made* by my mother.	Sometimes, even when the speaker knows who performs an action, s/he chooses to use the passive with the *by*-phrase because s/he wants to focus attention on the subject of a sentence. In (f): The focus of attention is on two rugs.

11-3 INDIRECT OBJECTS AS PASSIVE SUBJECTS

I.O. **D.O.** (a) Someone gave |‾*Mrs. Lee*‾| |‾an award.‾| (b) *Mrs. Lee* was given an award.	**I.O.** = *indirect object;* **D.O.** = *direct object* Either an indirect object or a direct object may become the subject of a passive sentence. (a), (b), (c), and (d) have the same meaning.
D.O. **I.O.** (c) Someone gave |‾*an award*‾| |‾to Mrs. Lee.‾| (d) *An award* was given to Mrs. Lee.	Notice in (d): When the direct object becomes the subject, *to* is usually kept in front of the indirect object.*

*The omission of *to* is more common in British English than American English: *An award was given Mrs. Lee.*

11-4 THE PASSIVE FORM OF MODALS AND PHRASAL MODALS

THE PASSIVE FORM:		modal*	+ *be* +	past participle	
(a)	Tom	*will*	*be*	*invited*	to the picnic.
(b)	The window	*can't*	*be*	*opened.*	
(c)	Children	*should*	*be*	*taught*	to respect their elders.
(d)		*May I*	*be*	*excused*	from class?
(e)	This book	*had better*	*be*	*returned*	to the library before Friday.
(f)	This letter	*ought to*	*be*	*sent*	before June 1st.
(g)	Mary	*has to*	*be*	*told*	about our change in plans.
(h)	Fred	*is supposed to*	*be*	*told*	about the meeting.

THE PAST-PASSIVE FORM:		modal + *have been* +		past participle	
(i)	The letter	*should*	*have been*	*sent*	last week.
(j)	This house	*must*	*have been*	*built*	over 200 years ago.
(k)	Jack	*ought to*	*have been*	*invited*	to the party.

*See Chapters 9 and 10 for a discussion of the form, meaning, and use of modals and phrasal modals.

11-5 STATIVE PASSIVE

(a) The door is *old*. (b) The door is *green*. (c) The door is *locked*.	In (a) and (b): *old* and *green* are adjectives. They describe the door. In (c): *locked* is a past participle. It is used as an adjective. It describes the door.
(d) I locked the door five minutes ago. (e) The door was locked by me five minutes ago. (f) Now the door *is locked*.	When the passive form is used to describe an existing situation or state, as in (c), (f), and (i), it is called the "stative passive." In the stative passive: • no action is taking place; the action happened earlier. • there is no *by*-phrase. • the past participle functions as an adjective.
(g) Ann broke the window yesterday. (h) The window was broken by Ann. (i) Now the window *is broken*.	
(j) I *am interested in* Chinese art. (k) He *is satisfied with* his job. (l) Ann *is married to* Alex.	Prepositions other than *by* can follow stative passive verbs. (See Chart 11-6, p. 59.)
(m) I don't know where I am. I *am lost*. (n) I can't find my purse. It *is gone*. (o) I *am finished with* my work. (p) I *am done with* my work.	(m) through (p) are examples of idiomatic usage of the passive form in common, everyday English. These sentences have no equivalent active sentences.

11-6 COMMON STATIVE PASSIVE VERBS + PREPOSITIONS

(a) I'm *interested in* Greek culture. (b) He's *worried about* losing his job.	Many stative passive verbs are followed by prepositions other than *by*.

COMMON STATIVE PASSIVE VERBS + PREPOSITIONS

be accustomed to
be acquainted with
be addicted to
be annoyed with, by
be associated with

be bored with, by

be cluttered with
be composed of
be concerned about
be connected to
be coordinated with
be covered with
be crowded with

be dedicated to
be devoted to
be disappointed in, with
be discriminated against
be divorced from
be done with
be dressed in

be engaged to
be equipped with
be excited about
be exhausted from
be exposed to

be filled with
be finished with
be frightened of, by

be gone from

be interested in
be involved in

be known for

be limited to
be located in

be made of
be married to

be opposed to

be pleased with
be prepared for
be protected from
be provided with

be qualified for

be related to
be remembered for

be satisfied with
be scared of, by

be terrified of, by
be tired of, from

be worried about

John's bald head *is protected from* the hot sun when he wears his hat.

11-7　THE PASSIVE WITH *GET*

GET* + *ADJECTIVE (a) I*'m getting hungry*. Let's eat soon. (b) You shouldn't eat so much. You*'ll get fat*. (c) I stopped working because I *got sleepy*.	***Get*** may be followed by certain adjectives.* ***Get*** gives the idea of change — the idea of becoming, beginning to be, growing to be. In (a): ***I'm getting hungry*** = I wasn't hungry before, but now I'm beginning to be hungry.
GET* + *PAST PARTICIPLE (d) I stopped working because I *got tired*. (e) They *are getting married* next month. (f) I *got worried* because he was two hours late.	***Get*** may also be followed by a past participle. The past participle functions as an adjective; it describes the subject. The passive with ***get*** is common in spoken English, but is often not appropriate in formal writing.

*Some of the common adjectives that follow ***get*** are:

angry	*chilly*	*fat*	*hungry*	*old*	*thirsty*
anxious	*cold*	*full*	*late*	*rich*	*warm*
bald	*dark*	*good*	*light*	*sick*	*well*
better	*dizzy*	*heavy*	*mad*	*sleepy*	*wet*
big	*empty*	*hot*	*nervous*	*tall*	*worse*
busy					

11-8　PARTICIPIAL ADJECTIVES

—The problem confuses the students. (a) It is *a confusing problem*. —The students are confused by the problem. (b) They are *confused students*.	The *present participle* serves as an adjective with an active meaning. The noun it modifies performs an action. In (a): The noun ***problem*** does something; it ***confuses***. Thus, it is described as a "confusing problem." The *past participle* serves as an adjective with a passive meaning. In (b): The students are confused by something. Thus, they are described as "confused students."
—The story amuses the children. (c) It is *an amusing story*. —The children are amused by the story. (d) They are *amused children*.	In (c): The noun ***story*** performs the action. In (d): The noun ***children*** receives the action.

CHAPTER 12
Noun Clauses

12-1 INTRODUCTION

independent clause (a) Sue lives in Tokyo. independent clause (b) Where does Sue live?	A clause is a group of words containing a subject and a verb.★ An *independent clause* (or *main clause*) is a complete sentence. It contains the main subject and verb of a sentence. Examples (a) and (b) are complete sentences. (a) is a statement, and (b) is a question.
dependent clause (c) where Sue lives	A *dependent clause* (or *subordinate clause*) is not a complete sentence. It must be connected to an independent clause. Example (c) is a dependent clause.
indep. cl. dependent cl. (d) I know *where Sue lives*.	Example (d) is a complete sentence. It has an independent clause with the main subject **(I)** and verb **(know)** of the sentence. **Where Sue lives** is a dependent clause connected to an independent clause. **Where Sue lives** is called a *noun clause*.
noun phrase (e) **His story** was interesting. noun clause (f) **What he said** was interesting.	A *noun phrase* is used as a subject or an object. A *noun clause* is used as a subject or an object. In other words, a noun clause is used in the same ways as a noun phrase. In (e): **His story** is a noun phrase. It is used as the subject of the sentence. In (f): **What he said** is a noun clause. It is used as the subject of the sentence. The noun clause has its own subject **(he)** and verb **(said)**.
noun phrase (g) I heard **his story**. noun clause (h) I heard **what he said**.	In (g): **his story** is a noun phrase. It is used as the object of the verb **heard**. In (h): **what he said** is a noun clause. It is used as the object of the verb **heard**.
noun phrase (i) I listened to **his story**. noun clause (j) I listened to **what he said**.	In (i): **his story** is a noun phrase. It is used as the object of the preposition **to**. In (j): **what he said** is a noun clause. It is used as the object of the preposition **to**.

★A *phrase* is a group of words that does NOT contain a subject and a verb.

★★See Appendix Unit B for more information about question words and question forms.

QUESTION	NOUN CLAUSE	
Where does she live? What did he say?` When do they arrive?	(a) I don't know *where she lives*. (b) I couldn't hear *what he said*. (c) Do you know *when they arrive?*	In (a): *where she lives* is the object of the verb *know*. In a noun clause, the subject precedes the verb. Do not use question word order in a noun clause. Notice: *does*, *did*, and *do* are used in questions, but not in noun clauses. See Appendix Unit B for more information about question words and question forms.
S **V** Who lives there? What happened? Who is at the door?	**S** **V** (d) I don't know *who lives there*. (e) Please tell me *what happened*. (f) I wonder *who is at the door*.	In (d): The word order is the same in both the question and the noun clause because *who* is the subject in both.
V **S** Who is she? Who are those men? Whose house is that?	**S** **V** (g) I don't know *who she is*. (h) I don't know *who those men are*. (i) I wonder *whose house that is*.	In (g): *she* is the subject of the question, so it is placed in front of the verb *be* in the noun clause.*
What did she say? What should they do?	(j) *What she said* surprised me. (k) *What they should do* is obvious.	In (j): *What she said* is the subject of the sentence. Notice in (k): A noun clause subject takes a singular verb (e.g., *is*).

*COMPARE: *Who is at the door?* = *who* is the subject of the question
              Who are those men? = *those men* is the subject of the question, so *be* is plural.

Sally wants to know
where this bus goes.

12-3 NOUN CLAUSES BEGINNING WITH *WHETHER* OR *IF*

YES/NO QUESTION	NOUN CLAUSE	
Will she come?	(a) I don't know *whether she will come.* I don't know *if she will come.*	When a yes/no question is changed to a noun clause, *whether* or *if* is used to introduce the clause.
Does he need help?	(b) I wonder *whether he needs help.* I wonder *if he needs help.*	(Note: *Whether* is more acceptable in formal English, but *if* is quite commonly used, especially in speaking.)
	(c) I wonder *whether or not* she will come. (d) I wonder *whether* she will come *or not.* (e) I wonder *if* she will come *or not.*	In (c), (d), and (e): Notice the patterns when *or not* is used.
	(f) *Whether she comes or not* is unimportant to me.	In (f): Notice that the noun clause is in the subject position.

12-4 QUESTION WORDS FOLLOWED BY INFINITIVES

(a) I don't know *what I should do.* (b) I don't know *what to do.* (c) Pam can't decide *whether she should go or stay home.* (d) Pam can't decide *whether to go or (to) stay home.* (e) Please tell me *how I can get to the bus station.* (f) Please tell me *how to get to the bus station.* (g) Jim told us *where we could find it.* (h) Jim told us *where to find it.*	Question words (*when, where, how, who, whom, whose, what, which*) and *whether* may be followed by an infinitive. Each pair of sentences in the examples has the same meaning. Notice that the meaning expressed by the infinitive is either *should* or *can/could*.

12-5 NOUN CLAUSES BEGINNING WITH *THAT*

STATEMENT	NOUN CLAUSE	
He is a good actor.	(a) I think *that he is a good actor.* (b) I think *he is a good actor.*	In (a): *that he is a good actor* is a noun clause. It is used as the object of the verb *think.*
The world is round.	(c) We know *(that) the world is round.*	The word *that*, when it introduces a noun clause, has no meaning in itself. It simply marks the beginning of the clause. Frequently it is omitted, as in (b), especially in speaking. (If used in speaking, it is unstressed.)
She doesn't understand spoken English.	(d) *That* she doesn't understand spoken English is obvious. (e) *It* is obvious *(that)* she doesn't understand *spoken English.*	In (d): The noun clause (*That she doesn't understand spoken English*) is the subject of the sentence. The word *that* is not omitted when it introduces a noun clause used as the subject of a sentence, as in (d) and (f).
The world is round.	(f) *That* the world is round is a fact. (g) *It* is a fact *that* the world is round.	More commonly, the word *it* functions as the subject and the noun clause is placed at the end of the sentence, as in (e) and (g).

12-6 QUOTED SPEECH

Quoted speech refers to reproducing words exactly as they were originally spoken.*
Quotation marks ("...") are used.**

QUOTING ONE SENTENCE (a) She said, *"My* brother is a student." (b) "My brother is a student," she said. (c) "My brother," she said, *"is* a student."	In (a): Use a comma after *she said*. Capitalize the first word of the quoted sentence. Put the final quotation marks outside the period at the end of the sentence. In (b): Use a comma, not a period, at the end of the quoted sentence when it precedes *she said*. In (c): If the quoted sentence is divided by *she said,* use a comma after the first part of the quote. Do not capitalize the first word after *she said*.
QUOTING MORE THAN ONE SENTENCE (d) *"My* brother is a student. He is attending a university," she said. (e) "My brother is a student," she said. *"He* is attending a university."	In (d): Quotation marks are placed at the beginning and end of the complete quote. Notice: There are no quotation marks after **student**. In (e): If *she said* comes between two quoted sentences, the second sentence begins with quotation marks and a capital letter.
QUOTING A QUESTION OR AN EXCLAMATION (f) She asked, "When will you be here?" (g) "When will you be here?" she asked. (h) She said, "Watch out!"	In (f): The question mark is inside the quotation marks. In (g): If a question mark is used, no comma is used before *she asked*. In (h): The exclamation point is inside the quotation marks.
(i) "My brother is a student," *said Anna*. "My brother," *said Anna,* "is a student."	In (i): The noun subject *(Anna)* follows **said**. A noun subject often follows the verb when the subject and verb come in the middle or at the end of a quoted sentence. (Note: A pronoun subject almost always precedes the verb. Very rare: *"My brother's a student," said she.*)
(j) "Let's leave," *whispered* Dave. (k) "Please help me," *begged* the unfortunate man. (l) "Well," Jack *began,* "it's a long story."	*Say* and *ask* are the most commonly used quote verbs. Some others: *add, agree, announce, answer, beg, begin, comment, complain, confess, continue, explain, inquire, promise, remark, reply, respond, shout, suggest, whisper.*

Quoted speech is also called "direct speech." *Reported speech* (discussed in Chart 12-7, p. 65) is also called "indirect speech."

**In British English, quotation marks are called "inverted commas" and can consist of either double marks (") or a single mark ('): She said, 'My brother is a student.'

"What's wrong, Officer?" I asked.
"Was I speeding?"

QUOTED SPEECH	REPORTED SPEECH	
(a) "I *watch* TV every day."	→ She said she *watched* TV every day.	*Reported speech* refers to using a noun clause to report what someone has said. No quotation marks are used.
(b) "I *am watching* TV."	→ She said she *was watching* TV.	
(c) "I *have watched* TV."	→ She said she *had watched* TV.	
(d) "I *watched* TV."	→ She said she *had watched* TV.	If the reporting verb (the main verb of the sentence, e.g., *said)* is simple past, the verb in the noun clause will usually also be in a past form, as in the examples.
(e) "I *had watched* TV."	→ She said she *had watched* TV.	
(f) "I *will watch* TV."	→ She said she *would watch* TV.	
(g) "I *am going to watch* TV."	→ She said she *was going to watch* TV.	
(h) "I *can watch* TV."	→ She said she *could watch* TV.	
(i) "I *may watch* TV."	→ She said she *might watch* TV.	
(j) "I *must watch* TV."	→ She said she *had to watch* TV.	
(k) "I *have to watch* TV."	→ She said she *had to watch* TV.	
(l) "I *should watch* TV."	→ She said she *should watch* TV.	In (l): ***should, ought to***, and ***might*** do not change to a past form.
"I *ought to watch* TV."	→ She said she *ought to watch* TV.	
"I *might watch* TV."	→ She said she *might watch* TV.	
(m) Immediate reporting: —What did the teacher just say? I didn't hear him. —He said he *wants* us to read Chapter Six. (n) Later reporting: —I didn't go to class yesterday. Did Mr. Jones make any assignments? —Yes. He said he *wanted* us to read Chapter Six.		Changing verbs to past forms in reported speech is common in both speaking and writing. However, sometimes in spoken English, no change is made in the noun clause verb, especially if the speaker is reporting something immediately or soon after it was said.
(o) "The world *is* round."	→ She said the world *is* round.	Also, sometimes the present tense is retained even in formal English when the reported sentence deals with a general truth, as in (o).
(p) "I *watch* TV every day."	→ She *says* she *watches* TV every day.	When the reporting verb is simple present, present perfect, or future, the noun clause verb is not changed.
(q) "I *watch* TV every day."	→ She *has said* that she *watches* TV every day.	
(r) "I *watch* TV every day."	→ She *will say* that she *watches* TV every day.	
(s) "*Watch* TV."	→ She *told* me *to watch* TV.★	In reported speech, an imperative sentence is changed to an infinitive. ***Tell*** is used instead of ***say*** as the reporting verb. See Chart 14-7, p. 77, for other verbs followed by an infinitive that are used to report speech.

★NOTE: ***Tell*** is immediately followed by a (pro)noun object, but ***say*** is not: *He told **me** he would be late. He said he would be late.* Also possible: *He said **to me** he would be late.*

12-8 USING THE SUBJUNCTIVE IN NOUN CLAUSES

(a) The teacher *demands* that we *be* on time. (b) I *insisted* that he *pay* me the money. (c) I *recommended* that she *not go* to the concert. (d) *It is important* that they *be told* the truth.	A subjunctive verb uses the simple form of a verb. It does not have present, past, or future forms; it is neither singular nor plural. Sentences with subjunctive verbs generally *stress importance or urgency*. A subjunctive verb is used in *that*-clauses that follow the verbs and expressions listed below. In (a): *be* is a subjunctive verb; its subject is *we*. In (b): *pay* (not *pays*, not *paid*) is a subjunctive verb; it is in its simple form, even though its subject (*he*) is singular. Negative: *not* + *simple form*, as in (c). Passive: *simple form of* *be* + *past participle*, as in (d).
(e) I *suggested* that she *see* a doctor. (f) I *suggested* that she *should see* a doctor.	*Should* is also possible after *suggest* and *recommend.**

COMMON VERBS AND EXPRESSIONS FOLLOWED BY THE SUBJUNCTIVE IN A NOUN CLAUSE

advise (that)	*propose (that)*	*it is essential (that)*	*it is critical (that)*
ask (that)	*recommend (that)*	*it is imperative (that)*	*it is necessary (that)*
demand (that)	*request (that)*	*it is important (that)*	*it is vital (that)*
insist (that)	*suggest (that)*		

*The subjunctive is more common in American English than British English. In British English, *should* + *simple form* is more usual than the subjunctive: *The teacher **insists** that we **should be** on time.*

12-9 USING -*EVER* WORDS

The following -*ever* words give the idea of "any." Each pair of sentences in the examples has the same meaning.

whoever	(a)	***Whoever*** wants to come is welcome. *Anyone who* wants to come is welcome.
who(m)ever	(b)	He makes friends easily with ***who(m)ever*** he meets.* He makes friends easily with *anyone who(m)* he meets.
whatever	(c)	He always says ***whatever*** comes into his mind. He always says *anything that* comes into his mind.
whichever	(d)	There are four good programs on TV at eight o'clock. We can watch ***whichever program*** (***whichever one***) you prefer. We can watch *any of the four programs that* you prefer.
whenever	(e)	You may leave ***whenever*** you wish. You may leave *at any time that* you wish.
wherever	(f)	She can go ***wherever*** she wants to go. She can go *anyplace that* she wants to go.
however	(g)	The students may dress ***however*** they please. The students may dress *in any way that* they please.

*In (b): ***whomever*** is the object of the verb ***meets***. In American English, ***whomever*** is rare and very formal. In British English, ***whoever*** (not ***whomever***) is used as the object form: *He makes friends easily with whoever he meets.*

CHAPTER 13
Adjective Clauses

13-1 INTRODUCTION

CLAUSE:	*A clause* is a group of words containing a subject and a verb.
INDEPENDENT CLAUSE:	*An independent clause* is a complete sentence. It contains the main subject and verb of a sentence. (It is also called "a main clause.")
DEPENDENT CLAUSE:	*A dependent clause* is not a complete sentence. It must be connected to an independent clause.
ADJECTIVE CLAUSE:	*An adjective clause* is a dependent clause that modifies a noun. It describes, identifies, or gives further information about a noun. (An adjective clause is also called "a relative clause.")
ADJECTIVE CLAUSE PRONOUNS:	An adjective clause uses pronouns to connect the dependent clause to the independent clause. The *adjective clause pronouns* are *who, whom, which, that,* and *whose*. (Adjective clause pronouns are also called "relative pronouns.")

13-2 ADJECTIVE CLAUSE PRONOUNS USED AS THE SUBJECT

I thanked the woman. ***She*** helped me. ↓ (a) I thanked the woman ***who*** *helped me.* (b) I thanked the woman ***that*** *helped me.*	In (a): ***I thanked the woman*** = an independent clause; ***who helped me*** = an adjective clause. The adjective clause modifies the noun ***woman***.
The book is mine. ***It*** is on the table. ↓ (c) The book ***which*** *is on the table* is mine. (d) The book ***that*** *is on the table* is mine.	In (a): ***who*** is the subject of the adjective clause. In (b): ***that*** is the subject of the adjective clause. Note: (a) and (b) have the same meaning. (c) and (d) have the same meaning.
	who = used for people ***which*** = used for things ***that*** = used for both people and things
(e) *INCORRECT: The book is mine that is on the table.*	An adjective clause closely follows the noun it modifies.

13-3 ADJECTIVE CLAUSE PRONOUNS USED AS THE OBJECT OF A VERB

The man was Mr. Jones. I saw **him**.	Notice in the examples: The adjective clause pronouns are placed at the beginning of the clause.
(a) The man **who(m)** *I saw* was Mr. Jones. (b) The man **that** *I saw* was Mr. Jones. (c) The man Ø *I saw* was Mr. Jones.	In (a): **who** is usually used instead of **whom**, especially in speaking. **Whom** is generally used only in very formal English.
The movie wasn't very good. We saw **it** last night.	In (c) and (f): An object pronoun is often omitted from an adjective clause. (A subject pronoun, however, may not be omitted.)
(d) The movie **which** *we saw last night* wasn't very good. (e) The movie **that** *we saw last night* wasn't very good. (f) The movie Ø *we saw last night* wasn't very good.	**who(m)** = used for people **which** = used for things **that** = used for both people and things
(g) *INCORRECT:* The man who(m) I saw *him* was Mr. Jones. The man that I saw *him* was Mr. Jones. The man I saw *him* was Mr. Jones.	In (g): The pronoun **him** must be removed. It is unnecessary because *who(m)*, *that*, or Ø functions as the object of the verb **saw**.

13-4 ADJECTIVE CLAUSE PRONOUNS USED AS THE OBJECT OF A PREPOSITION

She is the woman. I told you **about her**.	In very formal English, the preposition comes at the beginning of the adjective clause, as in (a) and (e). Usually, however, in everyday usage, the preposition comes after the subject and verb of the adjective clause, as in the other examples.
(a) She is the woman **about whom** *I told you.* (b) She is the woman **who(m)** *I told you* **about.** (c) She is the woman **that** *I told you* **about.** (d) She is the woman Ø *I told you* **about.**	
The music was good. We listened **to it** last night.	Note: If the preposition comes at the beginning of the adjective clause, only **whom** or **which** may be used. A preposition is never immediately followed by **that** or **who**.*
(e) The music **to which** *we listened* last night was good. (f) The music **which** *we listened* **to** last night was good. (g) The music **that** *we listened* **to** last night was good. (h) The music Ø *we listened* **to** last night was good.	

*INCORRECT: She is the woman *about who* I told you.
  INCORRECT: The music *to that* we listened last night was good.

13-5 USUAL PATTERNS OF ADJECTIVE CLAUSES

(a) USUAL: I like the people *who live next to me.* LESS USUAL: I like the people *that live next to me.*	In everyday informal usage, often one adjective clause pattern is used more commonly than another.* In (a): As a subject pronoun, *who* is more common than *that.*
(b) USUAL: I like books *that have good plots.* LESS USUAL: I like books *which have good plots.*	In (b): As a subject pronoun, *that* is more common than *which.*
(c) USUAL: I liked the people Ø *I met last night.* (d) USUAL: I liked the book Ø *I read last week.*	In (c) and (d): Object pronouns are commonly omitted, especially in speaking.

*See Chart 13-10, p. 71, for patterns of pronoun usage when an adjective clause requires commas.

13-6 USING *WHOSE*

I know the man.
His bicycle was stolen.
↓
(a) I know the man *whose bicycle was stolen.*
 	
The student writes well.
I read *her composition.*
↓
(b) The student *whose composition I read* writes well.
	Whose is used to show possession. It carries the same meaning as other possessive pronouns used as adjectives: *his, her, its,* and *their.* Like *his, her, its,* and *their, whose* is connected to a noun:
	    his bicycle → whose bicycle
	    her composition → whose composition
	Both *whose* and the noun it is connected to are placed at the beginning of the adjective clause. *Whose* cannot be omitted.

Mr. Catt has a painting. *Its value* is inestimable. ↓ (c) Mr. Catt has a painting *whose value is inestimable.*	*Whose* usually modifies people, but it may also be used to modify things, as in (c).

13-7 USING *WHERE* IN ADJECTIVE CLAUSES

The building is very old.
He lives *there (in that building).*
(a) The building *where*   *he lives*   is very old.
(b) The building *in which* *he lives*   is very old.
    The building *which*   *he lives in* is very old.
    The building *that*   *he lives in* is very old.
    The building Ø   *he lives in* is very old.
	Where is used in an adjective clause to modify a place (*city, country, room, house, etc.*).
	If *where* is used, a preposition is NOT included in the adjective clause, as in (a). If *where* is not used, the preposition must be included, as in (b).

13-8 USING *WHEN* IN ADJECTIVE CLAUSES

	I'll never forget the day. I met you **then** *(on that day)*.	***When*** is used in an adjective clause to modify a noun of time *(year, day, time, century, etc.)*.
(a)	I'll never forget the day ***when*** *I met you.*	The use of a preposition in an adjective clause that modifies a noun of time is somewhat different from that in other adjective clauses: a preposition is used preceding ***which***, as in (b). Otherwise, the preposition is omitted.
(b)	I'll never forget the day ***on which*** *I met you.*	
(c)	I'll never forget the day ***that*** *I met you.*	
(d)	I'll never forget the day Ø *I met you.*	

July is the month **when** the weather is the hottest.

13-9 USING ADJECTIVE CLAUSES TO MODIFY PRONOUNS

(a) There is ***someone*** *(whom) I want you to meet.* (b) ***Everything*** *he said* was pure nonsense. (c) ***Anybody*** *who wants to come* is welcome.	Adjective clauses can modify indefinite pronouns (e.g., *someone, everybody*). Object pronouns (e.g., *who(m), that, which*) are usually omitted in the adjective clause.
(d) Paula was ***the only one*** *I knew at the party.* (e) Scholarships are available for ***those*** *who need financial assistance.*	Adjective clauses can modify ***the one(s)*** and ***those***.*
(f) INCORRECT: *I who am a student at this school* come from a country in Asia. (g) It is ***I*** *who am responsible.* (h) ***He*** *who laughs last* laughs best.	Adjective clauses are almost never used to modify personal pronouns. Native English speakers would not write the sentence in (f). (g) is possible, but very formal and uncommon. (h) is a well-known saying in which ***he*** is used as an indefinite pronoun (meaning "anyone," "any person").

*An adjective clause with ***which*** can also be used to modify the demonstrative pronoun ***that***. For example:
We sometimes fear ***that which*** *we do not understand.*
The bread my mother makes is much better than ***that which*** *you can buy at a store.*

13-10 PUNCTUATING ADJECTIVE CLAUSES

General guidelines for the punctuation of adjective clauses:
(1) **DO NOT USE COMMAS IF** the adjective clause is necessary to identify the noun it modifies.★
(2) **USE COMMAS IF** the adjective clause simply gives additional information and is not necessary to identify the noun it modifies.★★

(a) ***The professor*** *who teaches Chemistry 101* is an excellent lecturer. (b) ***Professor Wilson,*** *who teaches Chemistry 101,* is an excellent lecturer.	In (a): No commas are used. The adjective clause is necessary to identify which professor is meant. In (b): Commas are used. The adjective clause is not necessary to identify Professor Wilson. We already know who he is: he has a name. The adjective clause simply gives additional information.
(c) ***Hawaii,*** *which consists of eight principal islands,* is a favorite vacation spot. (d) ***Mrs. Smith,*** *who is a retired teacher,* does volunteer work at the hospital.	Guideline: Use commas, as in (b), (c), and (d), if an adjective clause modifies a proper noun. (A proper noun begins with a capital letter.) Note: A comma reflects a pause in speech.
(e) ***The man*** $\begin{Bmatrix} who(m) \\ that \\ \varnothing \end{Bmatrix}$ *I met* teaches chemistry. (f) ***Mr. Lee,*** *whom I met yesterday,* teaches chemistry.	In (e): If no commas are used, any possible pronoun may be used in the adjective clause. Object pronouns may be omitted. In (f): When commas are necessary, the pronoun ***that*** may not be used (only ***who, whom, which, whose, where,*** and ***when*** may be used), and object pronouns cannot be omitted.
COMPARE THE MEANING (g) We took some children on a picnic. ***The children, who wanted to play soccer,*** ran to an open field as soon as we arrived at the park. (h) We took some children on a picnic. ***The children who wanted to play soccer*** ran to an open field as soon as we arrived at the park. The others played a different game.	In (g): The use of commas means that *all* of the children wanted to play soccer and *all* of the children ran to an open field. The adjective clause is used only to give additional information about the children. In (h): The lack of commas means that *only some* of the children wanted to play soccer. The adjective clause is used to identify which children ran to the open field.

★Adjective clauses that do not require commas are called "essential" or "restrictive" or "identifying."

★★Adjective clauses that require commas are called "nonessential" or "nonrestrictive" or "nonidentifying."

NOTE: Nonessential adjective clauses are more common in writing than in speaking.

13-11 USING EXPRESSIONS OF QUANTITY IN ADJECTIVE CLAUSES

In my class there are 20 students. *Most of **them** are from the Far East.* (a) In my class there are 20 students, *most of **whom*** are from Asia.	An adjective clause may contain an expression of quantity with **of**: *some of, many of, most of, none of, two of, half of, both of, neither of, each of, all of, several of, a few of, little of, a number of,* etc.
He gave several reasons. *Only a few of **them** were valid.* (b) He gave several reasons, *only a few of **which*** were valid.	The expression of quantity precedes the pronoun. Only **whom**, **which**, and **whose** are used in this pattern.
The teachers discussed Jim. *One of **his** problems was poor study habits.* (c) The teachers discussed Jim, *one of **whose** problems* was poor study habits.	Adjective clauses that begin with an expression of quantity are more common in writing than speaking. Commas are used.

13-12 USING NOUN + *OF WHICH*

We have an antique table. *The top of **it** has jade inlay.* (a) We have an antique table, ***the top of which*** has jade inlay.	An adjective clause may include *a noun + **of which*** (e.g., *the top of which*). This pattern carries the meaning of **whose** (e.g., *We have an antique table whose top has jade inlay.*). This pattern is used in an adjective clause that modifies a thing and occurs primarily in formal written English. A comma is used.

13-13 USING *WHICH* TO MODIFY A WHOLE SENTENCE

(a) Tom was late. (b) ***That*** surprised me. (c) Tom was late, ***which** surprised me.* (d) The elevator is out of order. (e) ***This*** is too bad. (f) The elevator is out of order, ***which** is too bad.*	The pronouns ***that*** and ***this*** can refer to the idea of a whole sentence which comes before. In (b): The word ***that*** refers to the whole sentence "Tom was late." Similarly, an adjective clause with ***which*** may modify the idea of a whole sentence. In (c): The word ***which*** refers to the whole sentence "Tom was late." Using ***which*** to modify a whole sentence is informal and occurs most frequently in spoken English. This structure is generally not appropriate in formal writing. Whenever it is written, however, it is preceded by a comma to reflect a pause in speech.

13-14 REDUCING ADJECTIVE CLAUSES TO ADJECTIVE PHRASES: INTRODUCTION

CLAUSE: *A clause* is a group of related words that contains a subject and a verb.
PHRASE: *A phrase* is a group of related words that does not contain a subject and a verb.

(a) ADJECTIVE CLAUSE: The girl *who is sitting next to me* is Maria. (b) ADJECTIVE PHRASE: The girl *sitting next to me* is Maria.	An adjective phrase is a reduction of an adjective clause. It modifies a noun. It does not contain a subject and verb. The adjective clause in (a) can be reduced to the adjective phrase in (b). (a) and (b) have the same meaning.
(c) CLAUSE: The boy *who is playing the piano* is Ben. (d) PHRASE: The boy *playing the piano* is Ben.	Only adjective clauses that have a subject pronoun—*who*, *which*, or *that*—are reduced to modifying adjective phrases.
(e) CLAUSE: The boy *(whom) I saw* was Tom. (f) PHRASE: *(none)*	The adjective clause in (e) cannot be reduced to an adjective phrase.

13-15 CHANGING AN ADJECTIVE CLAUSE TO AN ADJECTIVE PHRASE

(a) CLAUSE: The man *who is talking* to John is from Korea. PHRASE: The man Ø Ø *talking* to John is from Korea.	There are two ways in which an adjective clause is changed to an adjective phrase.
(b) CLAUSE: The ideas *which are presented* in that book are good. PHRASE: The ideas Ø Ø *presented* in that book are good. (c) CLAUSE: Ann is the woman *who is responsible* for the error. PHRASE: Ann is the woman Ø Ø *responsible* for the error. (d) CLAUSE: The books *that are on that shelf* are mine. PHRASE: The books Ø Ø *on that shelf* are mine.	1. If the adjective clause contains the *be* form of a verb, omit the pronoun and the *be* form, as in examples (a), (b), (c), and (d).
(e) CLAUSE: English has an alphabet *that consists* of 26 letters. PHRASE: English has an alphabet Ø *consisting* of 26 letters. (f) CLAUSE: Anyone *who wants* to come with us is welcome. PHRASE: Anyone Ø *wanting* to come with us is welcome.	2. If there is no *be* form of a verb in the adjective clause, it is sometimes possible to omit the subject pronoun and change the verb to its *-ing* form, as in (e) and (f).
(g) George Washington, *who was the first president of the United States,* was a wealthy colonist and a general in the army. (h) George Washington, *the first president of the United States,* was a wealthy colonist and a general in the army.	If the adjective clause requires commas, as in (g), the adjective phrase also requires commas, as in (h).
(i) *Paris, the capital of France,* is an exciting city. (j) I read a book by *Mark Twain, a famous American author.*	Adjective phrases in which a noun follows another noun, as in (h), (i), and (j), are called "appositives."

*If an adjective clause that contains *be* + *a single adjective* is changed, the adjective is moved to its normal position in front of the noun it modifies.
      CLAUSE: *Fruit that is fresh* tastes better than old, soft, mushy fruit.
  CORRECT PHRASE: *Fresh fruit* tastes better than old, soft, mushy fruit.
  INCORRECT PHRASE: Fruit fresh tastes better than old, soft, mushy fruit.

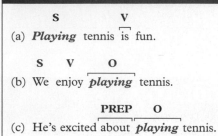

CHAPTER *14*
Gerunds and Infinitives, Part 1

14-1 GERUNDS: INTRODUCTION

$\overset{S}{}\qquad\overset{V}{}$ (a) **Playing** tennis is fun. $\overset{S}{}\quad\overset{V}{}\quad\overset{O}{}$ (b) We enjoy **playing** tennis. $\overset{PREP}{}\quad\overset{O}{}$ (c) He's excited about **playing** tennis.	A *gerund* is the *-ing* form of a verb used as a noun.* A gerund is used in the same ways as a noun, i.e., as a subject or as an object. In (a): **playing** is a gerund. It is used as the subject of the sentence. **Playing tennis** is a *gerund phrase*. In (b): **playing** is a gerund used as the object of the verb **enjoy**. In (c): **playing** is a gerund used as the object of the preposition **about**.

*COMPARE the uses of the *-ing* form of verbs:
  (1) **Walking** *is good exercise.*
      → **walking** = a gerund used as the subject of the sentence.
  (2) *Bob and Ann are* **playing** *tennis.*
      → **playing** = a present participle used as part of the present progressive tense.
  (3) *I heard some* **surprising** *news.*
      → **surprising** = a present participle used as an adjective.

14-2 USING GERUNDS AS THE OBJECTS OF PREPOSITIONS

(a) We talked **about going** to Canada for our vacation. (b) Sue is in charge **of organizing** the meeting. (c) I'm interested **in learning** more about your work.	A gerund is frequently used as the object of a preposition.
(d) I**'m used to sleeping** with the window open. (e) I**'m accustomed to sleeping*** with the window open. (f) I **look forward to going** home next month. (g) They **object to changing** their plans at this late date.	In (d) through (g): **to** is a preposition, not part of an infinitive form, so a gerund follows.
(h) We **talked about not going** to the meeting, but finally decided we should go.	Negative form: **not** precedes a gerund.

*Possible in British English: *I'm accustomed to sleep with the window open.*

14-3 COMMON PREPOSITION COMBINATIONS FOLLOWED BY GERUNDS

be excited
be worried } *about doing* it

complain
dream
talk
think } *about/of doing* it

apologize
blame (someone)
forgive (someone)
have an excuse
have a reason
be responsible
thank (someone) } *for doing* it

keep (someone)
prevent (someone)
prohibit (someone)
stop (someone) } *from doing* it

believe
be interested
participate
succeed } *in doing* it

be accused
be capable
for the purpose
be guilty
instead
take advantage
take care
be tired } *of doing* it

insist *on doing* it

be accustomed
in addition
be committed
be devoted
look forward
object
be opposed
be used } *to doing* it

14-4 COMMON VERBS FOLLOWED BY GERUNDS

(a) I $\underset{\text{verb}}{\overline{enjoy}}$ $\underset{\text{gerund}}{\overline{playing}}$ tennis.	Gerunds are used as the objects of certain verbs. In (a), *enjoy* is followed by a gerund *(playing)*. *Enjoy* is not followed by an infinitive. *INCORRECT:* I enjoy *to play* tennis. Common verbs that are followed by gerunds are given in the list below.
(b) Joe *quit smoking*. (c) Joe *gave up smoking*.	(b) and (c) have the same meaning. Some phrasal verbs,* e.g., *give up*, are followed by gerunds. These phrasal verbs are given in parentheses in the list below.

VERB + GERUND

enjoy	*quit (give up)*	*avoid*	*consider*
appreciate	*finish (get through)*	*postpone (put off)*	*discuss*
mind	*stop*****	*delay*	*mention*
		keep (keep on)	*suggest*

*A *phrasal verb* consists of a verb and a particle (a small word such as a preposition) that together have a special meaning. For example, *put off* means "postpone."

Stop can also be followed immediately by an infinitive of purpose *(in order to)*. See Chart 15-2, p. 82.
   COMPARE the following:
     (1) *stop + gerund:* When the professor entered the room, the students *stopped talking*. The room became quiet.
     (2) *stop + infinitive of purpose:* While I was walking down the street, I ran into an old friend. I *stopped to talk* to him.
       (I stopped walking *in order to talk* to him.)

14-5 *GO* + GERUND

(a) Did you *go shopping?* (b) We *went fishing* yesterday.	***Go*** is followed by a gerund in certain idiomatic expressions to express, for the most part, recreational activities.

GO + GERUND

go birdwatching	*go fishing**	*go sailing*	*go skinnydipping*
go boating	*go hiking*	*go shopping*	*go sledding*
go bowling	*go hunting*	*go sightseeing*	*go snorkeling*
go camping	*go jogging*	*go skating*	*go swimming*
go canoeing/kayaking	*go mountain climbing*	*go skateboarding*	*go tobogganing*
go dancing	*go running*	*go skiing*	*go window shopping*

*Also, in British English: *go angling*

14-6 SPECIAL EXPRESSIONS FOLLOWED BY *-ING*

(a) We *had fun*
We *had a good time* } *playing* volleyball.
	-ing forms follow certain special expressions:
	   have fun/a good time + *-ing*
	   have trouble/difficulty + *-ing*
	   have a hard time/difficult time + *-ing*

(b) I *had trouble* I *had difficulty* I *had a hard time* I *had a difficult time* } *finding* his house.	
(c) Sam *spends most of his time studying.* (d) I *waste a lot of time watching* TV.	***spend*** + *expression of time or money* + *-ing* ***waste*** + *expression of time or money* + *-ing*
(e) She *sat at her desk writing* a letter. (f) I *stood there wondering* what to do next. (g) He *is lying in bed reading* a novel.	***sit*** + *expression of place* + *-ing* ***stand*** + *expression of place* + *-ing* ***lie*** + *expression of place* + *-ing*
(h) When I walked into my office, I *found George using* my telephone. (i) When I walked into my office, I *caught a thief looking* through my desk drawers.	***find*** + *(pro)noun* + *-ing* ***catch*** + *(pro)noun* + *-ing* In (h) and (i): Both ***find*** and ***catch*** mean "discover." ***Catch*** often expresses anger or displeasure.

14-7   COMMON VERBS FOLLOWED BY INFINITIVES

VERB + INFINITIVE (a) I *hope to see* you again soon. (b) He *promised to be* here by ten. (c) He *promised not to be* late.	An *infinitive* = ***to*** + *the simple form of a verb (to see, to be, to go, etc.).* Some verbs are followed immediately by an infinitive, as in (a) and (b). See Group A below. Negative form: ***not*** precedes the infinitive, as in (c).
VERB + (PRO)NOUN + INFINITIVE (d) Mr. Lee *told me to be* here at ten o'clock. (e) The police *ordered the driver to stop.* (f) I *was told to be* here at ten o'clock. (g) The driver *was ordered to stop.*	Some verbs are followed by a (pro)noun and then an infinitive, as in (d) and (e). See Group B below. These verbs are followed immediately by an infinitive when they are used in the passive, as in (f) and (g).

(h) I *expect to pass* the test.
(i) I *expect Mary to pass* the test.
	Ask, expect, would like, want, and *need* may or may not be followed by a (pro)noun object.
	COMPARE
	   In (h): I think I will pass the test.
	   In (i): I think Mary will pass the test.

GROUP A: VERB + INFINITIVE

hope *to (do something)*	**promise** *to*	**seem** *to*	**expect** *to*
plan *to*	**agree** *to*	**appear** *to*	**would like** *to*
intend *to**	**offer** *to*	**pretend** *to*	**want** *to*
decide *to*	**refuse** *to*	**ask** *to*	**need** *to*

GROUP B: VERB + (PRO)NOUN + INFINITIVE

tell *someone to*	**permit** *someone to*	**force** *someone to*	**need** *someone to*
advise *someone to***	**allow** *someone to*	**ask** *someone to*	
encourage *someone to*	**warn** *someone to*	**expect** *someone to*	
remind *someone to*	**require** *someone to*	**would like** *someone to*	
invite *someone to*	**order** *someone to*	**want** *someone to*	

***Intend** is usually followed by an infinitive *(I intend to go to the meeting)*, but sometimes may be followed by a gerund *(I intend going to the meeting)* with no change in meaning.

A gerund is used after **advise (active) if there is no (pro)noun object.
   COMPARE:
     (1) He **advised buying** a Fiat.
     (2) He **advised me to buy** a Fiat. I **was advised to buy** a Fiat.

14-8 COMMON VERBS FOLLOWED BY EITHER INFINITIVES OR GERUNDS

Some verbs can be followed by either an infinitive or a gerund, sometimes with no difference in meaning, as in Group A below, and sometimes with a difference in meaning, as in Group B below.

GROUP A: VERB + INFINITIVE OR GERUND, WITH NO DIFFERENCE IN MEANING	The verbs in Group A may be followed by either an infinitive or a gerund with little or no difference in meaning.
begin　　*like*　　*hate* *start*　　*love*　　*can't stand* *continue*　*prefer**　*can't bear*	
(a) It *began to rain*. / It *began raining*. (b) I *started to work*. / I *started working*. (c) It *was beginning to rain*.	In (a): There is no difference between *began to rain* and *began raining*. If the main verb is progressive, an infinitive (not a gerund) is usually used, as in (c).
GROUP B: VERB + INFINITIVE OR GERUND, WITH A DIFFERENCE IN MEANING	The verbs in Group B may be followed by either an infinitive or a gerund, but the meaning is different.
remember　　*regret* *forget*　　　*try*	
(d) Judy always *remembers to lock* the door. (e) Sam often *forgets to lock* the door. (f) I *remember seeing* the Alps for the first time. The sight was impressive. (g) I'*ll never forget seeing* the Alps for the first time.	*Remember* + *infinitive* = remember to perform responsibility, duty, or task, as in (d). *Forget* + *infinitive* = forget to perform a responsibility, duty, or task, as in (e). *Remember* + *gerund* = remember (recall) something that happened in the past, as in (f). *Forget* + *gerund* = forget something that happened in the past, as in (g).**
(h) I *regret to tell* you that you failed the test. (i) I *regret lending* him some money. He never paid me back.	*Regret* + *infinitive* = regret to say, to tell someone, to inform someone of some bad news, as in (h). *Regret* + *gerund* = regret something that happened in the past, as in (i).
(j) I'*m trying to learn* English. (k) The room was hot. I *tried opening* the window, but that didn't help. So I *tried turning* on the fan, but I was still hot. Finally, I turned on the air conditioner.	*Try* + *infinitive* = make an effort, as in (j). *Try* + *gerund* = experiment with a new or different approach to see if it works, as in (k).

*Notice the patterns with **prefer**:
　　prefer + *gerund:* I **prefer staying** home **to going** to the concert.
　　prefer + *infinitive:* I'd **prefer to stay** home (rather) **than (to) go** to the concert.

****Forget** followed by a gerund usually occurs in a negative sentence or in a question: e.g., *I'll never forget, I can't forget, Have you ever forgotten,* and *Can you ever forget* are often followed by a gerund phrase.

14-9 REFERENCE LIST OF VERBS FOLLOWED BY GERUNDS

Verbs with a bullet (•) can also be followed by infinitives. See Chart 14-10.

1.	*admit*	He *admitted stealing* the money.
2.	*advise•*	She *advised waiting* until tomorrow.
3.	*anticipate*	I *anticipate having* a good time on vacation.
4.	*appreciate*	I *appreciated hearing* from them.
5.	*avoid*	He *avoided answering* my question.
6.	*can't bear•*	I *can't bear waiting* in long lines.
7.	*begin•*	It *began raining.*
8.	*complete*	I finally *completed writing* my term paper.
9.	*consider*	I *will consider going* with you.
10.	*continue•*	He *continued speaking.*
11.	*delay*	He *delayed leaving* for school.
12.	*deny*	She *denied committing* the crime.
13.	*discuss*	They *discussed opening* a new business.
14.	*dislike*	I *dislike driving* long distances.
15.	*enjoy*	We *enjoyed visiting* them.
16.	*finish*	She *finished studying* about ten.
17.	*forget•*	I'*ll never forget visiting* Napoleon's tomb.
18.	*hate•*	I *hate making* silly mistakes.
19.	*can't help*	I *can't help worrying* about it.
20.	*keep*	I *keep hoping* he will come.
21.	*like•*	I *like going* to movies.
22.	*love•*	I *love going* to operas.
23.	*mention*	She *mentioned going* to a movie.
24.	*mind*	*Would* you *mind helping* me with this?
25.	*miss*	I *miss being* with my family.
26.	*postpone*	Let's *postpone leaving* until tomorrow.
27.	*practice*	The athlete *practiced throwing* the ball.
28.	*prefer•*	Ann *prefers walking* to driving to work.
29.	*quit*	He *quit trying* to solve the problem.
30.	*recall*	I *don't recall meeting* him before.
31.	*recollect*	I *don't recollect meeting* him before.
32.	*recommend*	She *recommended seeing* the show.
33.	*regret•*	I *regret telling* him my secret.
34.	*remember•*	I *can remember meeting* him when I was a child.
35.	*resent*	I *resent her interfering* in my business.
36.	*resist*	I *couldn't resist eating* the dessert.
37.	*risk*	She *risks losing* all of her money.
38.	*can't stand•*	I *can't stand waiting* in long lines.
39.	*start•*	It *started raining.*
40.	*stop*	She *stopped going* to classes when she got sick.
41.	*suggest*	She *suggested going* to a movie.
42.	*tolerate*	She *won't tolerate cheating* during an examination.
43.	*try•*	I *tried changing* the light bulb, but the lamp still didn't work.
44.	*understand*	I *don't understand his leaving* school.

14-10 REFERENCE LIST OF VERBS FOLLOWED BY INFINITIVES

Verbs with a bullet (•) can also be followed by gerunds. See Chart 14-9.

A. VERBS FOLLOWED IMMEDIATELY BY AN INFINITIVE

1.	*afford*	I *can't afford to buy* it.	24.	*love•*	I *love to go* to operas.
2.	*agree*	They *agreed to help* us.	25.	*manage*	She *managed to finish* her work early.
3.	*appear*	She *appears to be* tired.	26.	*mean*	I *didn't mean to hurt* your feelings.
4.	*arrange*	I'll *arrange to meet* you at the airport.	27.	*need*	I *need to have* your opinion.
5.	*ask*	He *asked to come* with us.	28.	*offer*	They *offered to help* us.
6.	*can't bear•*	I *can't bear to wait* in long lines.	29.	*plan*	I *am planning to have* a party.
7.	*beg*	He *begged to come* with us.	30.	*prefer•*	Ann *prefers to walk* to work.
8.	*begin•*	It *began to rain*.	31.	*prepare*	We *prepared to welcome* them.
9.	*care*	I *don't care to see* that show.	32.	*pretend*	He *pretends not to understand*.
10.	*claim*	She *claims to know* a famous movie star.	33.	*promise*	I *promise not to be* late.
11.	*consent*	She finally *consented to marry* him.	34.	*refuse*	I *refuse to believe* his story.
12.	*continue•*	He *continued to speak*.	35.	*regret•*	I *regret to tell* you that you failed.
13.	*decide*	I *have decided to leave* on Monday.	36.	*remember•*	I *remembered to lock* the door.
14.	*demand*	I *demand to know* who is responsible.	37.	*seem*	That cat *seems to be* friendly.
15.	*deserve*	She *deserves to win* the prize.	38.	*can't stand•*	I *can't stand to wait* in long lines.
16.	*expect*	I *expect to enter* graduate school in the fall.	39.	*start•*	It *started to rain*.
17.	*fail*	She *failed to return* the book to the library on time.	40.	*struggle*	I *struggled to stay* awake.
18.	*forget•*	I *forgot to mail* the letter.	41.	*swear*	She *swore to tell* the truth.
19.	*hate•*	I *hate to make* silly mistakes.	42.	*threaten*	She *threatened to tell* my parents.
20.	*hesitate*	*Don't hesitate to ask* for my help.	43.	*try•*	I'm *trying to learn* English.
21.	*hope*	Jack *hopes to arrive* next week.	44.	*volunteer*	He *volunteered to help* us.
22.	*learn*	He *learned to play* the piano.	45.	*wait*	I *will wait to hear* from you.
23.	*like•*	I *like to go* to the movies.	46.	*want*	I *want to tell* you something.
			47.	*wish*	She *wishes to come* with us.

B. VERBS FOLLOWED BY A (PRO)NOUN + AN INFINITIVE

48.	*advise•*	She *advised me to wait* until tomorrow.	61.	*instruct*	He *instructed them to be* careful.
49.	*allow*	She *allowed me to use* her car.	62.	*invite*	Harry *invited the Johnsons to come* to his party.
50.	*ask*	I *asked John to help* us.	63.	*need*	We *needed Chris to help* us figure out the solution.
51.	*beg*	They *begged us to come*.	64.	*order*	The judge *ordered me to pay* a fine.
52.	*cause*	Her laziness *caused her to fail*.	65.	*permit*	He *permitted the children to stay* up late.
53.	*challenge*	She *challenged me to race* her to the corner.	66.	*persuade*	I *persuaded him to come* for a visit.
54.	*convince*	I couldn't *convince him to accept* our help.	67.	*remind*	She *reminded me to lock* the door.
55.	*dare*	He *dared me to do* better than he had done.	68.	*require*	Our teacher *requires us to be* on time.
56.	*encourage*	He *encouraged me to try* again.	69.	*teach*	My brother *taught me to swim*.
57.	*expect*	I *expect you to be* on time.	70.	*tell*	The doctor *told me to take* these pills.
58.	*forbid*	I *forbid you to tell* him.	71.	*urge*	I *urged her to apply* for the job.
59.	*force*	They *forced him to tell* the truth.	72.	*want*	I *want you to be* happy.
60.	*hire*	She *hired a boy to mow* the lawn.	73.	*warn*	I *warned you not to drive* too fast.

14-11 *IT* + INFINITIVE; GERUNDS AND INFINITIVES AS SUBJECTS

(a) ***It*** is difficult ***to learn*** a second language.	Often an infinitive phrase is used with ***it*** as the subject of a sentence. The word ***it*** refers to and has the same meaning as the infinitive phrase at the end of the sentence. In (a): ***It*** = *to learn a second language.*
(b) ***Learning*** a second language is difficult.	A gerund phrase is frequently used as the subject of a sentence, as in (b).
(c) ***To learn*** a second language is difficult.	An infinitive can also be used as the subject of a sentence, as in (c), but far more commonly an infinitive phrase is used with ***it***, as in (a).
(d) It is easy ***for young children*** to learn a second language. *Learning a second language is easy **for young children**.* *To learn a second language is easy **for young children**.*	The phrase ***for (someone)*** may be used to specify exactly who the speaker is talking about, as in (d).

It's fun ***to swim*** in a pool.
Swimming in a pool is fun.

CHAPTER 15
Gerunds and Infinitives, Part 2

15-1 INFINITIVE OF PURPOSE: *IN ORDER TO*

(a) He came here *in order to study* English. (b) He came here *to study* English.	*In order to* is used to express *purpose*. It answers the question "Why?" *In order* is often omitted, as in (b).
(c) *INCORRECT:* He came here *for studying* English. (d) *INCORRECT:* He came here *for to study* English. (e) *INCORRECT:* He came here *for study* English.	To express purpose, use *(in order) to*, not *for*, with a verb.*
(f) I went to the store *for* some bread. (g) I went to the store *to buy* some bread.	*For* can be used to express purpose, but it is a preposition and is followed by a noun object, as in (f).

*Exception: The phrase *be used for* expresses the typical or general purpose of a thing. In this case, the preposition *for* is followed by a gerund: *A saw is used for cutting* wood. Also possible: *A saw is used to cut* wood.

However, to talk about a particular thing and a particular situation, *be used* + *an infinitive* is used: *A chain saw was used to cut* (NOT *for cutting*) *down the old oak tree.*

15-2 ADJECTIVES FOLLOWED BY INFINITIVES

(a) We *were sorry to hear* the bad news. (b) I *was surprised to see* Tim at the meeting.	Certain adjectives can be immediately followed by infinitives, as in (a) and (b). In general, these adjectives describe a person (or persons), not a thing. Many of these adjectives describe a person's feelings or attitudes.

SOME COMMON ADJECTIVES FOLLOWED BY INFINITIVES

glad to (do it)	*sorry to★*	*ready to*	*careful to*	*surprised to★*
happy to	*sad to★*	*prepared to*	*hesitant to*	*amazed to★*
pleased to	*upset to★*	*anxious to*	*reluctant to*	*astonished to★*
delighted to	*disappointed to★*	*eager to*	*afraid to*	*shocked to★*
content to		*willing to*		*stunned to★*
relieved to	*proud to*	*motivated to*	*likely to*	
lucky to	*ashamed to*	*determined to*	*certain to*	
fortunate to				

*The expressions with asterisks are usually followed by infinitive phrases with verbs such as *see, learn, discover, find out, hear.*

15-3 USING INFINITIVES WITH *TOO* AND *ENOUGH*

COMPARE (a) That box is *too heavy* for Bob to lift. (b) That box is *very heavy,* but Bob can lift it.	In the speaker's mind, the use of *too* implies a negative result. In (a): *too heavy* = It is *impossible* for Bob to lift that box. In (b): *very heavy* = It is *possible but difficult* for Bob to lift that box.
(c) I am *strong enough to lift* that box. I can lift it. (d) I have *enough strength to lift* that box. (e) I have *strength enough to lift* that box.	*Enough* follows an adjective, as in (c). Usually *enough* precedes a noun, as in (d). In formal English, it may follow a noun, as in (e).

15-4 PASSIVE AND PAST FORMS OF INFINITIVES AND GERUNDS

FORMS

	SIMPLE	PAST
ACTIVE	to see seeing	to have seen having seen
PASSIVE	to be seen being seen	to have been seen having been seen

PAST INFINITIVE: *to have* + *past participle* (a) The rain seems *to have stopped*.	The event expressed by a past infinitive or past gerund happened before the time of the main verb. In (a): *The rain seems now to have stopped a few minutes ago.*★
PAST GERUND: *having* + *past participle* (b) I appreciate *having had* the opportunity to meet the king.	In (b): I met the king yesterday. *I appreciate now having had the opportunity to meet the king yesterday.*★
PAST INFINITIVE: *to be* + *past participle* (c) I didn't expect *to be invited* to his party.	In (c): *to be invited* is passive. The understood *by*-phrase is "by him": *I didn't expect to be invited by him.*
PAST GERUND: *being* + *past participle* (d) I appreciated *being invited* to your home.	In (d): *being invited* is passive. The understood *by*-phrase is "by you": *I appreciated being invited by you.*
PAST-PASSIVE INFINITIVE: *to have been* + *past participle* (e) Nadia is fortunate *to have been given* a scholarship.	In (e): Nadia was given a scholarship last month by her government. She is fortunate. *Nadia is fortunate now to have been given a scholarship last month by her government.*
PAST-PASSIVE GERUND: *having been* + *past participle* (f) I appreciate *having been told* the news.	In (f): I was told the news yesterday by someone. I appreciate that. *I appreciate now having been told the news yesterday by someone.*

★If the main verb is past, the action of the past infinitive or gerund happened before a time in the past:
*The rain **seemed to have stopped**.* = The rain seemed at six P.M. to have stopped before six P.M.
*I **appreciated having had** the opportunity to meet the king.* = I met the king in 1995. In 1997 I appreciated having had the opportunity to meet the king in 1995.

15-5 USING GERUNDS OR PASSIVE INFINITIVES FOLLOWING *NEED*

(a) I *need to borrow* some money. (b) John *needs to be told* the truth.	Usually an infinitive follows *need*, as in (a) and (b).
(c) The house *needs painting*. (d) The house *needs to be painted*.	In certain circumstances, a gerund may follow *need*. In this case, the gerund carries a passive meaning. Usually the situations involve fixing or improving something. (c) and (d) have the same meaning.

15-6 USING A POSSESSIVE TO MODIFY A GERUND

We came to class late. Mr. Lee complained about that fact. (a) FORMAL: Mr. Lee complained about *our coming* to class late.* (b) INFORMAL: Mr. Lee complained about *us coming* to class late.	In formal English, a possessive adjective (e.g., *our*) is used to modify a gerund, as in (a). In informal English, the object form of a pronoun (e.g., *us*) is frequently used, as in (b).
(c) FORMAL: Mr. Lee complained about *Mary's coming* to class late. (d) INFORMAL: Mr. Lee complained about *Mary coming* to class late.	In very formal English, a possessive noun (e.g., *Mary's*) is used to modify a gerund. The possessive form is often not used in informal English, as in (d).

Coming to class late occurred before Mr. Lee complained, so a past gerund is also possible: *Mr. Lee complained about our having come to class late.*

15-7 USING VERBS OF PERCEPTION

(a) I *saw* my friend *run* down the street. (b) I *saw* my friend *running* down the street. (c) I *heard* the rain *fall* on the roof. (d) I *heard* the rain *falling* on the roof.	Certain verbs of perception are followed by either *the simple form** or *the -ing form*** of a verb. There is often little difference in meaning between the two forms, except that the *-ing* form usually gives the idea of "while." In (b): I saw my friend while she was running down the street.
(e) When I walked into the apartment, I *heard* my roommate *singing* in the shower. (f) I *heard* a famous opera star *sing* at the concert last night.	Sometimes (not always) there is a clear difference between using the simple form or the *-ing* form. The use of the *-ing* form gives the idea that an activity is already in progress when it is perceived, as in (e): The singing was in progress when I first heard it. In (f): I heard the singing from beginning to end. It was not in progress when I first heard it.
VERBS OF PERCEPTION FOLLOWED BY THE SIMPLE FORM OR THE *-ING* FORM *see* *look at* *hear* *feel* *smell* *notice* *observe* *listen to* *watch*	

*The simple form of a verb = the infinitive form without "to." INCORRECT: I saw my friend *to run* down the street.

**The *-ing* form refers to the present participle.

15-8 USING THE SIMPLE FORM AFTER *LET* AND *HELP*

(a) My father *lets* me *drive* his car. (b) I *let* my friend *borrow* my bicycle. (c) *Let's go* to a movie.	*Let* is followed by the simple form of a verb, not an infinitive. *INCORRECT:* My father lets me *to drive* his car.
(d) My brother *helped* me *wash* my car. (e) My brother *helped* me *to wash* my car.	*Help* is often followed by the simple form of a verb, as in (d). An infinitive is also possible, as in (e). Both (d) and (e) are correct.

15-9 USING CAUSATIVE VERBS: *MAKE, HAVE, GET*

(a) I *made* my brother *carry* my suitcase. (b) I *had* my brother *carry* my suitcase. (c) I *got* my brother *to carry* my suitcase.	*Make, have,* and *get* can be used to express the idea that "X" causes "Y" to do something. When they are used as causative verbs, their meanings are similar but not identical. In (a): My brother had no choice. I insisted that he carry my suitcase. In (b): My brother carried my suitcase because I asked him to. In (c): I managed to persuade my brother to carry my suitcase.
FORMS X *makes* Y *do* something. (simple form) X *has* Y *do* something. (simple form) X *gets* Y *to do* something. (infinitive)	
CAUSATIVE *MAKE* (d) Mrs. Lee *made* her son *clean* his room. (e) Sad movies *make* me *cry*.	Causative *make* is followed by the simple form of a verb, not an infinitive. *(INCORRECT:* She made him *to clean* his room.) *Make* gives the idea that "X" **forces** "Y" to do something. In (d): Mrs. Lee's son had no choice.
CAUSATIVE *HAVE* (f) I *had* the plumber *repair* the leak. (g) Jane *had* the waiter *bring* her some tea.	Causative *have* is followed by the simple form of a verb, not an infinitive. *(INCORRECT:* I had him *to repair* the leak.) *Have* gives the idea that "X" **requests** "Y" to do something. In (f): The plumber repaired the leak because I asked him to.
CAUSATIVE *GET* (h) The students *got* the teacher *to dismiss* class early. (i) Jack *got* his friends *to play* soccer with him after school.	Causative *get* is followed by an infinitive. *Get* gives the idea that "X" **persuades** "Y" to do something. In (h): The students managed to persuade the teacher to let them leave early.
PASSIVE CAUSATIVES (j) I *had* my watch *repaired* (by someone). (k) I *got* my watch *repaired* (by someone).	The past participle is used after *have* and *get* to give a passive meaning. In this case, there is usually little or no difference in meaning between *have* and *get*. In (j) and (k): I caused my watch to be repaired by someone.

CHAPTER *16*
Coordinating Conjunctions

16-1 PARALLEL STRUCTURE

One use of a conjunction is to connect words or phrases that have the same grammatical function in a sentence. This use of conjunctions is called "parallel structure." The conjunctions used in this pattern are **and**, **but**, **or**, **nor**. These words are called "coordinating conjunctions."

(a) *Steve **and** his friend* are coming to dinner.	In (a): *noun + **and** + noun*
(b) Susan *raised* her hand ***and** snapped* her fingers.	In (b): *verb + **and** + verb*
(c) He *is waving* his arms ***and** (is) shouting* at us.	In (c): *verb + **and** + verb* (The second auxiliary may be omitted if it is the same as the first auxiliary.)
(d) These shoes are *old **but** comfortable*.	In (d): *adjective + **but** + adjective*
(e) He wants *to watch* TV ***or** (to) listen* to some music.	In (e): *infinitive + **or** + infinitive* (The second **to** is usually omitted.)
(f) *Steve, Joe, **and** Alice* are coming to dinner.	A parallel structure may contain more than two parts. In a series, commas are used to separate each unit.
(g) Susan *raised* her hand, *snapped* her fingers, ***and** asked* a question.	The final comma that precedes the conjunction is optional; also correct: *Steve, Joe and Alice* are coming to dinner.
(h) The colors in that fabric are *red, gold, black, **and** green*.	
(i) *INCORRECT: Steve, and Joe* are coming to dinner.	Note: No commas are used if there are only two parts to a parallel structure.

He gave her ***flowers on Sunday***,
candy on Monday,
and ***a ring on Tuesday***.

16-2 PAIRED CONJUNCTIONS: *BOTH . . . AND; NOT ONLY . . . BUT ALSO; EITHER . . . OR; NEITHER . . . NOR*

(a) ***Both*** *my mother* ***and*** *my sister* ***are*** here.	Two subjects connected by ***both . . . and*** take a plural verb, as in (a).
(b) ***Not only*** *my mother* ***but also*** *my sister* ***is*** here. (c) ***Not only*** *my sister* ***but also*** *my parents* ***are*** here. (d) ***Neither*** *my mother* ***nor*** *my sister* ***is*** here. (e) ***Neither*** *my sister* ***nor*** *my parents* ***are*** here.	When two subjects are connected by ***not only . . . but also***, ***either . . . or***, or ***neither . . . nor***, the subject that is closer to the verb determines whether the verb is singular or plural.
(f) The research project will take ***both*** *time* ***and*** *money*. (g) Yesterday it ***not only*** *rained* ***but (also)*** *snowed*. (h) I'll take ***either*** *chemistry* ***or*** *physics* next quarter. (i) That book is ***neither*** *interesting* ***nor*** *accurate*.	Notice the parallel structure in the examples. The same grammatical form should follow each part of the paired conjunctions.★ In (f): ***both*** + *noun* + ***and*** + *noun* In (g): ***not only*** + *verb* + ***but also*** + *verb* In (h): ***either*** + *noun* + ***or*** + *noun* In (i): ***neither*** + *adjective* + ***nor*** + *adjective*

★Paired conjunctions are also called "correlative conjunctions."

16-3 COMBINING INDEPENDENT CLAUSES WITH COORDINATING CONJUNCTIONS

(a) It was raining hard. There was a strong wind. (b) *INCORRECT PUNCTUATION:* It was raining hard**,** there was a strong wind.	Example (a) contains two *independent clauses* (i.e., two complete sentences). Notice the punctuation. A period,★ NOT A COMMA, is used to separate two independent clauses. The punctuation in (b) is not correct; the error in (b) is called "a run-on sentence."
(c) It was raining hard, ***and*** there was a strong wind. (d) It was raining hard ***and*** there was a strong wind. (e) It was raining hard. ***And*** there was a strong wind.	A *conjunction* may be used to connect two independent clauses. PUNCTUATION: Usually a comma immediately precedes the conjunction, as in (c). In short sentences, the comma is sometimes omitted, as in (d). In informal writing, a conjunction sometimes begins a sentence, as in (e).
(f) He was tired, ***so*** he went to bed. (g) The child hid behind his mother's skirt, ***for*** he was afraid of the dog. (h) She did not study, ***yet*** she passed the exam.	In addition to ***and***, ***but***, ***or***, and ***nor***, other conjunctions are used to connect two independent clauses: ***so*** (meaning "therefore, as a result") ***for*** (meaning "because") ***yet*** (meaning "but, nevertheless") A comma almost always precedes ***so***, ***for***, and ***yet*** when they are used as coordinating conjunctions.★★

★ In British English, a period is called "a full stop."

★★ ***So***, ***for***, and ***yet*** have other meanings in other structures: e.g., *He is not* ***so*** *tall as his brother.* (***so*** = ***as***) *We waited* ***for*** *the bus.* (***for*** = a preposition) *She hasn't arrived* ***yet***. (***yet*** = an adverb meaning "up to this time")

CHAPTER 17
Adverb Clauses

17-1 INTRODUCTION

(a) *When we were in New York,* we saw several plays. (b) We saw several plays *when we were in New York.*	*When we were in New York* is an adverb clause. PUNCTUATION: When an adverb clause precedes an independent clause, as in (a), a comma is used to separate the clauses. When the adverb clause follows, as in (b), usually no comma is used.
(c) *Because he was sleepy,* he went to bed. (d) He went to bed *because he was sleepy.*	Like ***when***, ***because*** introduces an adverb clause. *Because he was sleepy* is an adverb clause.
(e) INCORRECT: *When we were in New York. We saw several plays.* (f) INCORRECT: *He went to bed. Because he was sleepy.*	Adverb clauses are dependent clauses. They cannot stand alone as a sentence in written English. They must be connected to an independent clause.*

SUMMARY LIST OF WORDS USED TO INTRODUCE ADVERB CLAUSES**

TIME		CAUSE AND EFFECT	CONTRAST	CONDITION
after	*by the time (that)*	*because*	*even though*	*if*
before	*once*	*now that*	*although*	*unless*
when	*as/so long as*	*since*	*though*	*only if*
while	*whenever*			*whether or not*
as	*every time (that)*		DIRECT CONTRAST	*even if*
as soon as	*the first time (that)*		*while*	*in case*
since	*the last time (that)*		*whereas*	*in the event that*
until	*the next time (that)*			

*See Chart 13-1, p. 67, for the definition of dependent and independent clauses.

**Words that introduce adverb clauses are called "subordinating conjunctions."

17-2 USING ADVERB CLAUSES TO SHOW CAUSE AND EFFECT

because	(a) *Because he was sleepy,* he went to bed. (b) He went to bed *because he was sleepy.*	An adverb clause may precede or follow the independent clause. Notice the punctuation in (a) and (b).
now that	(c) *Now that the semester is over,* I'm going to rest a few days and then take a trip. (d) Jack lost his job. *Now that he's unemployed,* he can't pay his bills.	*Now that* means "because now." In (c): *Now that the semester is over* means "because the semester is now over." *Now that* is used for present causes of present or future situations.
since	(e) *Since Monday is a holiday,* we don't have to go to work. (f) *Since you're a good cook and I'm not,* you should cook the dinner.	When *since* is used to mean "because," it expresses a known cause; it means "because it is a fact that" or "given that it is true that." Cause and effect sentences with *since* say: "Given the fact that X is true, Y is the result." In (e): "Given the fact that Monday is a holiday, we don't have to go to work." Note: *Since* has two meanings. One is "because." It is also used in time clauses: e.g., *Since I came here, I have met many people.* See Chart 5-2, p. 25.

17-3 EXPRESSING CONTRAST (UNEXPECTED RESULT): USING *EVEN THOUGH*

(a) *Because* the weather was cold, I *didn't go* swimming. (b) *Even though* the weather was cold, I *went* swimming. (c) *Because* I wasn't tired, I *didn't go* to bed. (d) *Even though* I wasn't tired, I *went* to bed.	*Because* is used to express expected results. *Even though* is used to express unexpected results. Note: Like *because*, *even though* introduces an adverb clause.

17-4 SHOWING DIRECT CONTRAST: *WHILE* AND *WHEREAS*

(a) Mary is rich, *while John is poor.* (b) John is poor, *while Mary is rich.* (c) Mary is rich, *whereas John is poor.* (d) *Whereas Mary is rich,* John is poor.	*While* and *whereas* are used to show direct contrast: "this" is exactly the opposite of "that." *While* and *whereas* may be used with the idea of either clause with no difference in meaning. *Whereas* mostly occurs in formal written English. Note: A comma is usually used even if the adverb clause comes second.
COMPARE (e) *While I was studying,* the phone rang.	*While* is also used in time clauses and means "during the time that," as in (e). See Chart 5-2, p. 25.

17-5 EXPRESSING CONDITIONS IN ADVERB CLAUSES: *IF*-CLAUSES

(a) *If it rains*, the streets get wet.	*If*-clauses (also called "adverb clauses of condition") present possible conditions. The main clause expresses results. In (a): POSSIBLE CONDITION = *it rains* RESULT = *the streets get wet*
(b) *If it **rains** tomorrow*, I will take my umbrella.	A present tense, not a future tense, is used in an *if*-clause even though the verb in the *if*-clause may refer to a future event or situation, as in (b).★

WORDS THAT INTRODUCE ADVERB CLAUSES OF CONDITION (*IF*-CLAUSES)

if	*in case*	*unless*
whether or not	*in the event that*	*only if*
even if		

★See Chapter 20 for uses of other verb forms in sentences with *if*-clauses.

17-6 ADVERB CLAUSES OF CONDITION: USING *WHETHER OR NOT* AND *EVEN IF*

WHETHER OR NOT (a) I'm going to go swimming tomorrow *whether or not it is cold*. (OR: *whether it is cold or not*.)	*Whether or not* expresses the idea that neither this condition nor that condition matters; the result will be the same. In (a): "If it is cold, I'm going swimming. If it is not cold, I'm going swimming. I don't care about the temperature. It doesn't matter."
EVEN IF (b) I have decided to go swimming tomorrow. *Even if the weather is cold*, I'm going to go swimming.	Sentences with *even if* are close in meaning to those with *whether or not*. *Even if* gives the idea that a particular condition does not matter. The result will not change.

17-7 ADVERB CLAUSES OF CONDITION: USING *IN CASE* AND *IN THE EVENT THAT*

(a) I'll be at my uncle's house *in case you (should) need to reach me*. (b) *In the event that you (should) need to reach me*, I'll be at my uncle's house.	*In case* and *in the event that* express the idea that something probably won't happen, but it might. *In case/in the event that* means "if by chance this should happen." Notes: *In the event that* is more formal than *in case*. The use of *should* in the adverb clause emphasizes the speaker's uncertainty that something will happen.

17-8 ADVERB CLAUSES OF CONDITION: USING *UNLESS*

(a) I'll go swimming tomorrow *unless it's cold*. (b) I'll go swimming tomorrow *if it isn't cold*.	*unless = if . . . not* In (a): *unless it's cold* means "if it isn't cold." (a) and (b) have the same meaning.

17-9 ADVERB CLAUSES OF CONDITION: USING *ONLY IF*

(a) The picnic will be canceled *only if it rains*. If it's windy, we'll go on the picnic. If it's cold, we'll go on the picnic. If it's damp and foggy, we'll go on the picnic. If it's unbearably hot, we'll go on the picnic.	*Only if* expresses the idea that there is only one condition that will cause a particular result.
(b) *Only if* it rains *will the picnic be canceled*.	When *only if* begins a sentence, the subject and verb of the main clause are inverted, as in (b).* No commas are used.

*Other subordinating conjunctions and prepositional phrases fronted by *only* at the beginning of a sentence require subject-verb inversion in the main clause:

Only when the teacher dismisses us *can we stand* and *leave* the room.
Only after the phone rang *did I realize* that I had fallen asleep in my chair.
Only in my hometown *do I feel* at ease.

CHAPTER 18

Reduction of Adverb Clauses to Modifying Adverbial Phrases

18-1 INTRODUCTION

(a) ADVERB CLAUSE:	*While **I was walking** to class,* I ran into an old friend.	In Chapter 13, we discussed changing adjective clauses to modifying phrases (see Chart 13-13, p. 72). Some adverb clauses may also be changed to modifying phrases, and the ways in which the changes are made are the same:
(b) MODIFYING PHRASE:	*While **walking** to class,* I ran into an old friend.	
(c) ADVERB CLAUSE:	*Before **I left** for work,* I ate breakfast.	1. Omit the subject of the dependent clause and the ***be*** form of the verb, as in (b). OR
(d) MODIFYING PHRASE:	*Before **leaving** for work,* I ate breakfast.	2. If there is no ***be*** form of a verb, omit the subject and change the verb to **-*ing***, as in (d).
(e) CHANGE POSSIBLE:	*While **I was sitting** in class, **I** fell asleep.* *While **sitting** in class, **I** fell asleep.*	An adverb clause can be changed to a modifying phrase **only when the subject of the adverb clause and the subject of the main clause are the same**. A *modifying adverbial phrase* that is the reduction of an adverb clause *modifies the subject* of the main clause.
(f) CHANGE POSSIBLE:	*While **Ann was sitting** in class, **she** fell asleep. (clause)* *While **sitting** in class, **Ann** fell asleep.*	
(g) NO CHANGE POSSIBLE:	*While **the teacher** was lecturing to the class, **I** fell asleep.*★	No reduction (i.e., change) is possible if the subjects of the adverb clause and the main clause are different, as in (g) and (h).
(h) NO CHANGE POSSIBLE:	*While **we** were walking home, **a frog** hopped across the road in front of us.*	
(i) INCORRECT:	*While walking home, a frog hopped across the road in front of us.*	In (i): *While walking home* is called a "dangling modifier" or a "dangling participle," i.e., a modifier that is incorrectly "hanging alone" without an appropriate noun or pronoun subject to modify.
(j) INCORRECT:	*While watching TV last night,* the phone rang.	

★*While lecturing to the class, **I** fell asleep* means "While **I** was lecturing to the class, **I** fell asleep."

18-2 CHANGING TIME CLAUSES TO MODIFYING ADVERBIAL PHRASES

(a) CLAUSE: **Since Maria came** to this country, she has made many friends. (b) PHRASE: **Since coming** to this country, Maria has made many friends.	Adverb clauses beginning with **after**, **before**, **while**, and **since** can be changed to modifying adverbial phrases.
(c) CLAUSE: **After he (had) finished** his homework, Peter went to bed. (d) PHRASE: **After finishing** his homework, Peter went to bed. (e) PHRASE: **After having finished** his homework, Peter went to bed.	In (c): There is no difference in meaning between *After he finished* and *After he had finished*. (See Chart 3-3, p. 19.) In (d) and (e): There is no difference in meaning between *After finishing* and *After having finished*.
(f) PHRASE: Peter went to bed **after finishing** his homework.	A modifying adverbial phrase may follow the main clause, as in (f).

18-3 EXPRESSING THE IDEA OF "DURING THE SAME TIME" IN MODIFYING ADVERBIAL PHRASES

(a) **While I was walking** down the street, **I** ran into an old friend. (b) **While walking** down the street, **I** ran into an old friend. (c) **Walking** down the street, **I** ran into an old friend. (d) **Hiking** through the woods yesterday, **we** saw a bear. (e) **Pointing** to the sentence on the board, **the teacher** explained the meaning of modifying phrases.	Sometimes **while** is omitted but the **-ing** phrase at the beginning of the sentence gives the same meaning (i.e., "during the same time"). (a), (b), and (c) have the same meaning.

18-4 EXPRESSING CAUSE AND EFFECT IN MODIFYING ADVERBIAL PHRASES

(f) **Because she needed** some money to buy a book, **Sue** cashed a check. (g) **Needing** some money to buy a book, **Sue** cashed a check. (h) **Because he lacked** the necessary qualifications, **he** was not considered for the job. (i) **Lacking** the necessary qualifications, **he** was not considered for the job.	Often an **-ing** phrase at the beginning of a sentence gives the meaning of "because." (f) and (g) have the same meaning. **Because** is not included in a modifying phrase. It is omitted, but the resulting phrase expresses a cause and effect relationship, as in (g) and (i).
(j) **Having seen** that movie before, **I don't want** to go again. (k) **Having seen** that movie before, **I didn't want** to go again.	**Having** + *past participle* gives the meaning not only of "because" but also of "before."
(l) **Because she was unable** to afford a car, **she** bought a bicycle. (m) **Being unable** to afford a car, **she** bought a bicycle. (n) **Unable** to afford a car, **she** bought a bicycle.	A form of **be** in the adverb clause may be changed to **being**. The use of **being** makes the cause and effect relationship clear. (l), (m), and (n) have the same meaning.

18-5 USING *UPON* + *-ING* IN MODIFYING ADVERBIAL PHRASES

(a) ***Upon reaching*** the age of 21, I received my inheritance. (b) ***When I reached*** the age of 21, I received my inheritance.	Modifying adverbial phrases beginning with ***upon*** + ***-ing*** usually have the same meaning as adverb clauses introduced by ***when***. (a) and (b) have the same meaning.
(c) ***On reaching*** the age of 21, I received my inheritance.	***Upon*** can be shortened to ***on***. (a), (b), and (c) all have the same meaning.

Upon looking *in his wallet,* Alex discovered he didn't have enough money to pay the bill.

CHAPTER 19
Connectives That Express Cause and Effect, Contrast, and Condition

19-1 USING *BECAUSE OF* AND *DUE TO*

(a) ***Because*** *the weather was cold,* we stayed home.	***Because*** introduces an adverb clause; it is followed by a subject and verb, as in (a).
(b) ***Because of*** *the cold weather,* we stayed home. (c) ***Due to*** *the cold weather,* we stayed home.	***Because of*** and ***due to*** are phrasal prepositions; they are followed by a noun object, as in (b) and (c).
(d) ***Due to the fact that*** *the weather was cold,* we stayed home.	Sometimes, usually in more formal writing, ***due to*** is followed by a noun clause introduced by ***the fact that***.
(e) We stayed home *because of the cold weather.* We stayed home *due to the cold weather.* We stayed home *due to the fact that the weather was cold.*	Like adverb clauses, these phrases can also follow the main clause, as in (e).

19-2 USING TRANSITIONS TO SHOW CAUSE AND EFFECT: *THEREFORE* AND *CONSEQUENTLY*

(a) Al failed the test because he didn't study. (b) Al didn't study. ***Therefore,*** he failed the test. (c) Al didn't study. ***Consequently,*** he failed the test.	(a), (b), and (c) have the same meaning. ***Therefore*** and ***consequently*** mean "as a result." In grammar, they are called *transitions* (or *conjunctive adverbs*). Transitions connect the ideas between two sentences.

(d) Al didn't study. ***Therefore,*** he failed the test.
 (e) Al didn't study. He, ***therefore,*** failed the test.
 (f) Al didn't study. He failed the test, ***therefore***.
 	
 POSITIONS OF A TRANSITION
 	
     transition + s + v (+ rest of sentence)
     s + ***transition*** + v (+ rest of sentence)
     s + v (+ rest of sentence) + ***transition***
	A transition occurs in the second of two related sentences. Notice the patterns and punctuation in the examples. A period (NOT a comma) is used at the end of the first sentence.* The transition has several positions in the second sentence. The transition is separated from the rest of the sentence by commas.

(g) Al didn't study, ***so*** he failed the test.	COMPARE: A *transition* (e.g., ***therefore***) has several possible positions within the second sentence of the pair, as in (d), (e), and (f). A *conjunction* (e.g., ***so***) has only one possible position: between the two sentences. (See Chart 16-3, p. 87.) ***So*** cannot move around in the second sentence as ***therefore*** can.

*A semicolon is also possible in this situation. See the footnote to Chart 19-3, p. 96.

19-3 SUMMARY OF PATTERNS AND PUNCTUATION

ADVERB CLAUSE	(a) **Because** *it was hot,* we went swimming. (b) We went swimming **because** *it was hot.*	An *adverb clause* may precede or follow an independent clause. PUNCTUATION: A comma is used if the adverb clause comes first.
PREPOSITION	(c) **Because** *of the hot weather,* we went swimming. (d) We went swimming **because of** *the hot weather.*	A *preposition* is followed by a noun object, not by a subject and verb. PUNCTUATION: A comma is usually used if the prepositional phrase precedes the subject and verb of the independent clause.
TRANSITION	(e) It was hot. ***Therefore,*** *we went swimming.* (f) It was hot. *We,* ***therefore,*** *went swimming.* (g) It was hot. *We went swimming,* ***therefore.***	A *transition* is used with the second sentence of a pair. It shows the relationship of the second idea to the first idea. A transition is movable within the second sentence. PUNCTUATION: A period is used between the two independent clauses.* A comma may NOT be used to separate the clauses. Commas are usually used to set the transition off from the rest of the sentence.
CONJUNCTION	(h) It was hot, ***so*** *we went swimming.*	A conjunction comes between two independent clauses. PUNCTUATION: Usually a comma is used immediately in front of a conjunction.

*A semicolon (;) may be used instead of a period between the two independent clauses.

> *It was hot; therefore, we went swimming.*
> *It was hot; we, therefore, went swimming.*
> *It was hot; we went swimming, therefore.*

In general, a semicolon can be used instead of a period between any two sentences that are closely related in meaning.

Example: *Peanuts are not nuts; they are beans.* Notice that a small letter, not a capital letter, immediately follows a semicolon.

Because most 15th-century Europeans believed the world was flat, many sailors were afraid they might sail off the end of the world.

19-4 OTHER WAYS OF EXPRESSING CAUSE AND EFFECT: *SUCH . . . THAT* AND *SO . . . THAT*

(a) Because the weather was nice, we went to the zoo. (b) It was ***such nice weather that*** we went to the zoo. (c) The weather was ***so nice that*** we went to the zoo.	Examples (a), (b), and (c) have the same meaning.
(d) It was ***such good coffee that*** I had another cup. (e) It was ***such a foggy day that*** we couldn't see the road.	***Such . . . that*** encloses a modified noun: ***such*** + *adjective* + *noun* + ***that***
(f) The coffee is ***so hot that*** I can't drink it. (g) I'm ***so hungry that*** I could eat a horse. (h) She speaks ***so fast that*** I can't understand her. (i) He walked ***so quickly that*** I couldn't keep up with him.	***So . . . that*** encloses an adjective or adverb: $so + \begin{Bmatrix} adjective \\ or \\ adverb \end{Bmatrix} + that$
(j) She made ***so many mistakes that*** she failed the exam. (k) He has ***so few friends that*** he is always lonely. (l) She has ***so much money that*** she can buy whatever she wants. (m) He had ***so little trouble*** with the test ***that*** he left twenty minutes early.	***So . . . that*** is used with ***many***, ***few***, ***much***, and ***little***.
(n) It was ***such a good book*** *(that)* I couldn't put it down. (o) I was ***so hungry*** *(that)* I didn't wait for dinner to eat something.	Sometimes, primarily in speaking, ***that*** is omitted.

19-5 EXPRESSING PURPOSE: USING *SO THAT*

(a) I turned off the TV ***in order to*** *enable my roommate to study in peace and quiet.*	***In order to*** expresses *purpose.* (See Chart 15-1, p. 82.) In (a): I turned off the TV for a purpose. The purpose was to make it possible for my roommate to study in peace and quiet.
(b) I turned off the TV ***so (that)*** *my roommate could study in peace and quiet.*	***So that*** also expresses *purpose.** It expresses the same meaning as ***in order to***. The word "that" is often omitted, especially in speaking.
SO THAT + *CAN* or *COULD* (c) I'm going to cash a check ***so that I can*** *buy my textbooks.* (d) I cashed a check ***so that I could*** *buy my textbooks.*	***So that*** is often used instead of ***in order to*** when the idea of ability is being expressed. ***Can*** is used in the adverb clause for a present/future meaning. In (c): *so that I can buy = in order to be able to buy.* ***Could*** is used after ***so that*** in past sentences.**
SO THAT + *WILL* / SIMPLE PRESENT or *WOULD* (e) I'll take my umbrella ***so that I won't*** *get wet.* (f) I'll take my umbrella ***so that I don't*** *get wet.* (g) Yesterday I took my umbrella ***so that I wouldn't*** *get wet.*	In (e): *so that I won't get wet = in order to make sure that I won't get wet.* In (f): It is sometimes possible to use the simple present after ***so that*** in place of ***will***; the simple present expresses a future meaning. ***Would*** is used in past sentences; as in (g).

*NOTE: ***In order that*** has the same meaning as ***so that*** but is less commonly used.
  Example: *I turned off the TV **in order that** my roommate could study in peace and quiet.*
  Both ***so that*** and ***in order that*** introduce adverb clauses. It is unusual, but possible, to put these adverb clauses at the beginning of a sentence: ***So that** my roommate could study in peace and quiet, I turned off the TV.*

Also possible but less common: the use of ***may* or ***might*** in place of ***can*** or ***could***: e.g., *I cashed a check **so that I might** buy my textbooks.*

19-6 SHOWING CONTRAST (UNEXPECTED RESULT)

All these sentences have the same meaning. The idea of cold weather is contrasted with the idea of going swimming. Usually if the weather is cold, one does not go swimming, so going swimming in cold weather is an "unexpected result." It is surprising that the speaker went swimming in cold weather.

ADVERB CLAUSES	even though although though	(a) *Even though it was cold*, I went swimming. (b) *Although it was cold*, I went swimming. (c) *Though it was cold*, I went swimming.
CONJUNCTIONS	but . . . anyway but . . . still yet . . . still	(d) It was cold, *but* I went swimming *anyway*. (e) It was cold, *but* I *still* went swimming. (f) It was cold, *yet* I *still* went swimming.
TRANSITIONS	nevertheless nonetheless however . . . still	(g) It was cold. *Nevertheless*, I went swimming. (h) It was cold; *nonetheless*, I went swimming. (i) It was cold. *However*, I *still* went swimming.
PREPOSITIONS	despite in spite of despite the fact that in spite of the fact that	(j) I went swimming *despite* the cold weather. (k) I went swimming *in spite of* the cold weather. (l) I went swimming *despite the fact that* the weather was cold. (m) I went swimming *in spite of the fact that* the weather was cold.

19-7 SHOWING DIRECT CONTRAST

All of the sentences have the same meaning.

ADVERB CLAUSES	while whereas	(a) Mary is rich, *while John is poor*. (b) John is poor, *while Mary is rich*. (c) Mary is rich, *whereas John is poor*. (d) *Whereas Mary is rich*, John is poor.
CONJUNCTION	but	(e) Mary is rich, *but* John is poor. (f) John is poor, *but* Mary is rich.
TRANSITIONS	however on the other hand	(g) Mary is rich; *however*, John is poor. (h) John is poor; Mary is rich, *however*. (i) Mary is rich. John, *on the other hand*, is poor. (j) John is poor. Mary, *on the other hand*, is rich.

19-8 EXPRESSING CONDITIONS: USING *OTHERWISE* AND *OR (ELSE)*

ADVERB CLAUSE	(a) **If** *I don't eat breakfast,* I get hungry. (b) You'll be late **if** *you don't hurry.* (c) You'll get wet **unless** *you take your umbrella.*	**If** and **unless** state conditions that produce certain results. (See Charts 17-5 and 17-8, pp. 90 and 91.)
TRANSITION	(d) I always eat breakfast. **Otherwise,** I get hungry during class. (e) You'd better hurry. **Otherwise,** you'll be late. (f) Take your umbrella. **Otherwise,** you'll get wet.	**Otherwise** expresses the idea "if the opposite is true, then there will be a certain result." In (d): **otherwise** = *if I don't eat breakfast.*
CONJUNCTION	(g) I always eat breakfast, **or** *(else)* I get hungry during class. (h) You'd better hurry, **or** *(else)* you'll be late. (i) Take your umbrella, **or** *(else)* you'll get wet.	**Or else** and **otherwise** have the same meaning.

19-9 SUMMARY OF CONNECTIVES: CAUSE AND EFFECT, CONTRAST, CONDITION

	ADVERB CLAUSE WORDS		TRANSITIONS	CONJUNCTIONS	PREPOSITIONS
CAUSE AND EFFECT	*because* *since* *now that*	*so (that)*	*therefore* *consequently*	*so* *for*	*because of* *due to*
CONTRAST	*even though* *although* *though*	*whereas* *while*	*however* *nevertheless* *nonetheless* *on the other hand*	*but (. . . anyway)* *yet (. . . still)*	*despite* *in spite of*
CONDITION	*if* *unless* *only if* *even if* *whether or not*	*in case* *in the event that*	*otherwise*	*or (else)*	

CHAPTER 20

Conditional Sentences and Wishes

20-1 OVERVIEW OF BASIC VERB FORMS USED IN CONDITIONAL SENTENCES

SITUATION	*IF*-CLAUSE	RESULT CLAUSE	EXAMPLES
True in the present/future	simple present	simple present *will* + *simple form*	If I *have* enough time, I *watch* TV every evening. If I *have* enough time, I *will watch* TV later on tonight.
Untrue in the present/future	simple past	*would* + *simple form*	If I *had* enough time, I *would watch* TV now or later on.
Untrue in the past	past perfect	*would have* + *past participle*	If I *had had* enough time, I *would have watched* TV yesterday.

20-2 TRUE IN THE PRESENT OR FUTURE

(a) If I *don't eat* breakfast, I always *get* hungry during class.

(b) Water *freezes* OR *will freeze* if the temperature *reaches* 32°F/0°C.

(c) If I *don't eat* breakfast tomorrow morning, I *will get* hungry during class.

(d) If it *rains*, we *should stay* home.
 If it *rains*, I *might decide* to stay home.
 If it *rains*, we *can't go*.
 If it *rains*, we*'re going to stay* home.

(e) If anyone *calls*, please *take* a message.

In conditional sentences that express true, factual ideas in the present/future, the *simple present* (not the simple future) is used in the *if*-clause.

The result clause has various possible verb forms. A result clause verb can be:
1. the *simple present*, to express a habitual activity or situation, as in (a).
2. either the *simple present* or the *simple future*, to express an established, predictable fact or general truth, as in (b).
3. the *simple future*, to express a particular activity or situation in the future, as in (c).
4. *modals* and *phrasal modals* such as ***should***, ***might***, ***can***, ***be going to***, as in (d).*
5. an imperative verb, as in (e).

(f) If anyone ***should*** call, please take a message.

Sometimes ***should*** is used in an *if*-clause. It indicates a little more uncertainty than the use of the simple present, but basically the meaning of examples (e) and (f) is the same.

*See Chart 9-1, p. 43, for a list of modals and phrasal modals.

20-3 UNTRUE (CONTRARY TO FACT) IN THE PRESENT OR FUTURE

(a) If I *taught* this class, I *wouldn't give* tests. (b) If he *were* here right now, he *would help* us. (c) If I *were* you, I *would accept* their invitation.	In (a): In truth, I don't teach this class. In (b): In truth, he is not here right now. In (c): In truth, I am not you. Note: *Were* is used for both singular and plural subjects. *Was* (with *I, he, she, it*) is sometimes used in informal speech: *If I was you, I'd accept their invitation.*
COMPARE (d) If I had enough money, I *would* buy a car. (e) If I had enough money, I *could* buy a car.	In (d): The speaker wants a car, but doesn't have enough money. *Would* expresses desired or predictable results. In (e): The speaker is expressing one possible result. *Could* = *would be able to*. *Could* expresses possible options.

If I *were* a bird, I *wouldn't want* to spend my whole life in a cage.

20-4 UNTRUE (CONTRARY TO FACT) IN THE PAST

(a) If you *had told* me about the problem, I *would have helped* you. (b) If they *had studied*, they *would have passed* the exam. (c) If I *hadn't slipped* on the stairs, I *wouldn't have broken* my arm.	In (a): In truth, you did not tell me about it. In (b): In truth, they did not study. Therefore, they failed the exam. In (c): In truth, I slipped on the stairs. I broke my arm. Note: The auxiliary verbs are almost always contracted in speech. "If you'd told me, I would've helped you (OR I'd've helped you)."*
COMPARE (d) If I had had enough money, I *would have bought* a car. (e) If I had had enough money, I *could have bought* a car.	In (d): *would* expresses a desired or predictable result. In (e): *could* expresses a possible option; *could have bought = would have been able to buy.*

*In casual, informal speech, some native speakers sometimes use *would have* in an *if*-clause: *If you would've told me about the problem, I would've helped you.* This verb form usage is generally considered not to be grammatically correct standard English, but it occurs fairly commonly.

20-5 USING PROGRESSIVE VERB FORMS IN CONDITIONAL SENTENCES

Notice the use of progressive verb forms in these examples. Even in conditional sentences, progressive verb forms are used in progressive situations. (See Chart 1-2, p. 2, for a discussion of progressive verbs.)

(a) TRUE:	It *is raining* right now, so I *will not go for* a walk.	
(b) CONDITIONAL:	If it *were not raining* right now, I *would go* for a walk.	
(c) TRUE:	I *am not living* in Chile. I *am not working* at a bank.	
(d) CONDITIONAL:	If I *were living* in Chile, I *would be working* at a bank.	
(e) TRUE:	It *was raining* yesterday afternoon, so I *did not go* for a walk.	
(f) CONDITIONAL:	If it *had not been raining*, I *would have gone* for a walk.	
(g) TRUE:	I *was not living* in Chile last year. I *was not working* at a bank.	
(h) CONDITIONAL:	If I *had been living* in Chile last year, I *would have been working* at a bank.	

20-6 USING "MIXED TIME" IN CONDITIONAL SENTENCES

Frequently the time in the *if*-clause and the time in the result clause are different: one clause may be in the present and the other in the past. Notice that past and present times are mixed in these sentences.

(a) TRUE:	I *did not eat* breakfast several hours ago, so I *am* hungry now.
(b) CONDITIONAL:	If I *had eaten* breakfast several hours ago, I *would not be* hungry now.
	(past) *(present)*
(c) TRUE:	He *is not* a good student. He *did not study* for the test yesterday.
(d) CONDITIONAL:	If he *were* a good student, he *would have studied* for the test yesterday.
	(present) *(past)*

20-7 OMITTING *IF*

(a) *Were I* you, I wouldn't do that. (b) *Had I known*, I would have told you. (c) *Should anyone call*, please take a message.	With *were*, *had* (past perfect), and *should*, sometimes *if* is omitted and the subject and verb are inverted. In (a): *Were I you* = *if I were you.* In (b): *Had I known* = *if I had known.* In (c): *Should anyone call* = *if anyone should call.*

20-8 IMPLIED CONDITIONS

(a) I **would have gone** with you, *but I had to study*. (b) I never **would have succeeded** *without your help*.	Often the *if*-clause is implied, not stated. Conditional verbs are still used in the result clause. In (a): the implied condition = *if I hadn't had to study*. In (b): the implied condition = *if you hadn't helped me*.
(c) She ran; *otherwise*, she **would have missed** her bus.	Conditional verbs are frequently used following ***otherwise***. In (c), the implied *if*-clause = *if she had not run*.

20-9 USING *AS IF/AS THOUGH*

(a) It looks **like** *rain*. (b) It looks **as if** *it is going to rain*. (c) It looks **as though** *it is going to rain*. (d) It looks **like** *it is going to rain*. (informal)	Notice in (a): **like** is followed by a noun object. Notice in (b) and (c): **as if** and **as though** are followed by a clause. Notice in (d): **like** is followed by a clause. This use of **like** is common in informal English, but is not generally considered appropriate in formal English; **as if** or **as though** is preferred. (a), (b), (c), and (d) all have the same meaning.

"TRUE" STATEMENT (FACT)	VERB FORM AFTER *AS IF/AS THOUGH*	
(e) He **is not** a child.	She talked to him *as if* he **were** a child.	Usually the idea following **as if/as though** is "untrue." In this case, verb usage is similar to that in conditional sentences.
(f) She **did not take** a shower with her clothes on.	When she came in from the rainstorm, she looked *as if* she **had taken** a shower with her clothes on.	
(g) He **has met** her.	He acted *as though* he **had never met** her.	
(h) She **will be** here.	She spoke *as if* she **wouldn't be** here.	

I know a farmer who talks to his animals **as if/as though** they were people.

20-10 VERB FORMS FOLLOWING *WISH*

Wish is used when the speaker wants reality to be different, to be exactly the opposite.

	"TRUE" STATEMENT	VERB FORM FOLLOWING *WISH*	
A wish about the future	(a) She **will not tell** me. (b) He **isn't going to be** here. (c) She **can't come** tomorrow.	I *wish* (that) she **would tell** me. I *wish* he **were going to be** here. I *wish* she **could come** tomorrow.	*Wish* is followed by a noun clause. (See Chart 12-5, p. 63.) Past verb forms, similar to those in conditional sentences, are used in the noun clause. For example, in (a): **would**, the past form of **will**, is used to make a wish about the future. In (d): the simple past (**knew**) is used to make a wish about the present. In (g): the past perfect (**had come**) is used to make a wish about the past.
A wish about the present	(d) I **don't know** French. (e) It **is raining** right now. (f) I **can't speak** Japanese.	I *wish* I **knew** French. I *wish* it **weren't raining** right now. I *wish* I **could speak** Japanese.	
A wish about the past	(g) John **didn't come**. (h) Mary **couldn't come**.	I *wish* John **had come**.* I *wish* Mary **could have come**.	

*Sometimes in very informal speaking: *I wish John **would have come**.*

20-11 USING *WOULD* TO MAKE WISHES ABOUT THE FUTURE

(a) It is raining. I *wish* it **would stop**. *(I want it to stop raining.)* (b) I'm expecting a call. I *wish* the phone **would ring**. *(I want the phone to ring.)*	**Would** is usually used to indicate that the speaker wants something to happen or someone other than the speaker to do something in the future. The wish may or may not come true (be realized).
(c) It's going to be a good party. I *wish* you **would come**. (d) We're going to be late. I *wish* you **would hurry**.	In (c) and (d): **I wish you would** . . . is often used to make a request.

APPENDIX
Supplementary Grammar Units

UNIT A: Basic Grammar Terminology

A-1 SUBJECTS, VERBS, AND OBJECTS

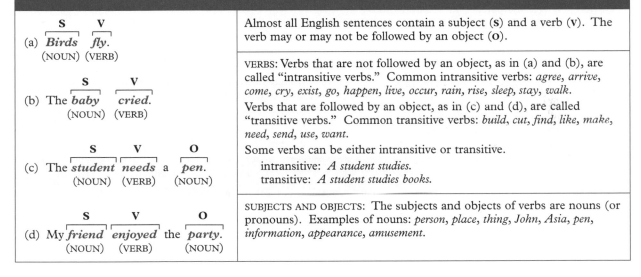

Almost all English sentences contain a subject (**s**) and a verb (**v**). The verb may or may not be followed by an object (**o**).

VERBS: Verbs that are not followed by an object, as in (a) and (b), are called "intransitive verbs." Common intransitive verbs: *agree, arrive, come, cry, exist, go, happen, live, occur, rain, rise, sleep, stay, walk.*

Verbs that are followed by an object, as in (c) and (d), are called "transitive verbs." Common transitive verbs: *build, cut, find, like, make, need, send, use, want.*

Some verbs can be either intransitive or transitive.

    intransitive: *A student studies.*
    transitive: *A student studies books.*

SUBJECTS AND OBJECTS: The subjects and objects of verbs are nouns (or pronouns). Examples of nouns: *person, place, thing, John, Asia, pen, information, appearance, amusement.*

A-2 PREPOSITIONS AND PREPOSITIONAL PHRASES

COMMON PREPOSITIONS

about	*at*	*beyond*	*into*	*since*	*up*
above	*before*	*by*	*like*	*through*	*upon*
across	*behind*	*despite*	*near*	*throughout*	*with*
after	*below*	*down*	*of*	*till*	*within*
against	*beneath*	*during*	*off*	*to*	*without*
along	*beside*	*for*	*on*	*toward(s)*	
among	*besides*	*from*	*out*	*under*	
around	*between*	*in*	*over*	*until*	

(a) **S** **V** **PREP** **O of PREP** The student studies *in* the *library*. (NOUN)	An important element of English sentences is the prepositional phrase. It consists of a preposition (**PREP**) and its object (**O**). The object of a preposition is a noun or pronoun. In (a): ***in the library*** is a prepositional phrase.
(b) **S** **V** **O** **PREP** **O of PREP** We enjoyed the party *at* *your* *house*. (NOUN)	
(c) We went ***to the zoo*** ***in the afternoon***. (place) (time) (d) ***In the afternoon***, we went to the zoo.	In (c): In most English sentences, "place" comes before "time." In (d): Sometimes a prepositional phrase comes at the beginning of a sentence.

A-3 ADJECTIVES

(a) Ann is an ***intelligent*** *student*.
                  (ADJECTIVE)   (NOUN)
(b) The ***hungry*** *child* ate fruit.
        (ADJECTIVE) (NOUN)
	Adjectives describe nouns. In grammar, we say that adjectives modify nouns. The word "modify" means "change a little." Adjectives give a little different meaning to a noun: *intelligent student, lazy student, good student.* Examples of adjectives: *young, old, rich, beautiful, brown, French, modern.*

(c) I saw some ***beautiful*** pictures. *INCORRECT*: beautifuls pictures	An adjective is neither singular nor plural. A final ***-s*** is never added to an adjective.

A-4 ADVERBS

(a) He walks **quickly**. 　　　　　(ADVERB) (b) She opened the door **quietly**. 　　　　　　　　　　　(ADVERB)	Adverbs modify verbs. Often they answer the question *"How?"* In (a): *How does he walk?* Answer: *Quickly.* Adverbs are often formed by adding *-ly* to an adjective. 　*adjective:* **quick** 　*adverb:*　**quickly**
(c) I am **extremely** *happy*. 　　(ADVERB) (ADJECTIVE)	Adverbs are also used to modify adjectives, i.e., to give information about adjectives, as in (c).
(d) Ann will come **tomorrow**. 　　　　　　　　　　(ADVERB)	Adverbs are also used to express time or frequency. Examples: *tomorrow, today, yesterday, soon, never, usually, always, yet.*
MIDSENTENCE ADVERBS (e) Ann **always** *comes* on time. (f) Ann *is* **always** on time. (g) Ann *has* **always** *come* on time. (h) *Does she* **always** *come* on time?	Some adverbs may occur in the middle of a sentence. Midsentence adverbs have usual positions; they 　(1) come in front of simple present and simple past verbs (except **be**), as in (e); 　(2) follow **be** (simple present and simple past), as in (f); 　(3) come between a helping verb and a main verb, as in (g). In a question, a midsentence adverb comes directly after the subject, as in (h).

COMMON MIDSENTENCE ADVERBS

ever	*usually*	*generally*	*seldom*	*never*	*already*
always	*often*	*sometimes*	*rarely*	*not ever*	*finally*
	frequently	*occasionally*	*hardly ever*		*just* *probably*

The young couple had **never** seen such a dilapidated house. They **quickly** decided not to buy it.

A-5 THE VERB *BE*

(a) John *is* **a student**. 　　(BE)　　(NOUN) (b) John *is* **intelligent**. 　　(BE)　　(ADJ) (c) John *was* **at the library**. 　　(BE)　　(PREP. PHRASE)	A sentence with *be* as the main verb has three basic patterns: In (a): *be* + *a noun* In (b): *be* + *an adjective* In (c): *be* + *a prepositional phrase*
(d) Mary *is* writing a letter. (e) They *were* listening to some music. (f) That letter *was* written by Alice.	*Be* is also used as an auxiliary verb in progressive verb tenses and in the passive. In (d): *is* = *auxiliary*; *writing* = *main verb*

TENSE FORMS OF *BE*

	SIMPLE PRESENT	SIMPLE PAST	PRESENT PERFECT
SINGULAR	*I* **am** *you* **are** *he, she, it* **is**	*I* **was** *you* **were** *he, she, it* **was**	*I* **have been** *you* **have been** *he, she, it* **has been**
PLURAL	*we, you, they* **are**	*we, you, they* **were**	*we, you, they* **have been**

The woman behind the perfume counter *is* a sales clerk. The man *is* buying some perfume from her.

A-6 LINKING VERBS

(a) The soup　　*smells*　　*good*. 　　(LINKING VERB)　(ADJECTIVE) (b) This food *tastes delicious*. (c) The children *feel happy*. (d) The weather *became cold*.	Other verbs like *be* that may be followed immediately by an adjective are called "linking verbs." An adjective following a linking verb describes the subject of a sentence.* Common verbs that may be followed by an adjective: • *feel, look, smell, sound, taste* • *appear, seem* • *become* (and *get, turn, grow* when they mean "become")

*COMPARE:
   (1) *The man looks angry.* → An adjective *(angry)* follows **look**. The adjective describes the subject *(the man)*. **Look** has the meaning of "appear."
   (2) *The man looked at me angrily.* → An adverb *(angrily)* follows **look at**. The adverb describes the action of the verb. **Look at** has the meaning of "regard, watch."

UNIT B: Questions

B-1 FORMS OF YES/NO AND INFORMATION QUESTIONS

A yes/no question = a question that may be answered by *yes* or *no*.
A: Does he live in Chicago?
B: Yes, he does. OR No, he doesn't.

An information question = a question that asks for information by using a question word.
A: Where does he live?
B: In Chicago.

Question word order = *(Question word) + helping verb + subject + main verb*
Notice that the same subject-verb order is used in both yes/no and information questions.

(QUESTION WORD)	HELPING VERB	SUBJECT	MAIN VERB	(REST OF SENTENCE)	
(a)	*Does*	*she*	*live*	there?	If the verb is in the simple present, use ***does*** (with *he, she, it*) or ***do*** (with *I, you, we, they*) in the question. If the verb is simple past, use ***did***. Notice: The main verb in the question is in its simple form; there is no final ***-s*** or ***-ed***.
(b) Where	*does*	*she*	*live?*		
(c)	*Do*	*they*	*live*	there?	
(d) Where	*do*	*they*	*live?*		
(e)	*Did*	*he*	*live*	there?	
(f) Where	*did*	*he*	*live?*		
(g)	*Is*	*he*	*living*	there?	If the verb has an auxiliary (a helping verb), the same auxiliary is used in the question. There is no change in the form of the main verb. If the verb has more than one auxiliary, only the first auxiliary precedes the subject, as in (m) and (n).
(h) Where	*is*	*he*	*living?*		
(i)	*Have*	*they*	*lived*	there?	
(j) Where	*have*	*they*	*lived?*		
(k)	*Can*	*Mary*	*live*	there?	
(l) Where	*can*	*Mary*	*live?*		
(m)	*Will*	*he*	*be living*	there?	
(n) Where	*will*	*he*	*be living?*		
(o) Who	Ø	Ø	*lives*	there?	If the question word is the subject, usual question word order is not used; ***does, do***, and ***did*** are not used. The verb is in the same form in a question as it is in a statement. Statement: *Tom came.* Question: *Who came?*
(p) Who	*can*	Ø	*come?*		
(q)	*Are*	*they*	Ø	there?	Main verb ***be*** in the simple present *(am, is, are)* and simple past *(was, were)* precedes the subject. It has the same position as a helping verb.
(r) Where	*are*	*they?*	Ø		
(s)	*Was*	*Jim*	Ø	there?	
(t) Where	*was*	*Jim?*	Ø		

B-2 QUESTION WORDS

	QUESTION	ANSWER	
WHEN	(a) **When** did they arrive? **When** will you come?	Yesterday. Next Monday.	**When** is used to ask questions about *time*.
WHERE	(b) **Where** is she? **Where** can I find a pen?	At home. In that drawer.	**Where** is used to ask questions about *place*.
WHY	(c) **Why** did he leave early? **Why** aren't you coming with us?	Because he's ill. I'm tired.	**Why** is used to ask questions about *reason*.
HOW	(d) **How** did you come to school? **How** does he drive?	By bus. Carefully.	**How** generally asks about *manner*.
	(e) **How much** money does it cost? **How many** people came?	Ten dollars. Fifteen.	**How** is used with **much** and **many**.
	(f) **How old** are you? **How cold** is it? **How soon** can you get here? **How fast** were you driving?	Twelve. Ten below zero. In ten minutes. 50 miles an hour.	**How** is also used with adjectives and adverbs.
	(g) **How long** has he been here? **How often** do you write home? **How far** is it to Miami from here?	Two years. Every week. 500 miles.	**How long** asks about *length of time*. **How often** asks about *frequency*. **How far** asks about *distance*.

Why didn't you bring the directions?

Whose idea was it to take this route?

Where's our map?

Who can we call if we get lost?

What are we supposed to do now?

Which road should I take?

How do we get to Maple Street from here?

WHO	(h) **Who** can answer that question? **Who** came to visit you?	I can. Jane and Eric.	**Who** is used as the subject of a question. It refers to people.
	(i) **Who** is coming to dinner tonight? **Who** wants to come with me?	Ann, Bob, and Al. We do.	**Who** is usually followed by a singular verb even if the speaker is asking about more than one person.
WHOM	(j) **Who(m)** did you see? **Who(m)** are you visiting? (k) **Who(m)** should I talk *to*? *To* **whom** should I talk? *(formal)*	I saw George. My relatives. The secretary.	**Whom** is used as the object of a verb or preposition. In everyday spoken English, **whom** is rarely used; **who** is used instead. **Whom** is used only in formal questions. Note: **Whom**, not **who**, is used if preceded by a preposition.
WHOSE	(l) **Whose** book did you borrow? **Whose** key is this? (**Whose** is this?)	David's. It's mine.	**Whose** asks questions about *possession*.
WHAT	(m) **What** made you angry? **What** went wrong?	His rudeness. Everything.	**What** is used as the subject of a question. It refers to things.
	(n) **What** do you need? **What** did Alice buy? (o) **What** did he talk *about*? *About* **what** did he talk? *(formal)*	I need a pencil. A book. His vacation.	**What** is also used as an object.
	(p) **What kind of** soup is that? **What kind of** shoes did he buy?	It's bean soup. Sandals.	**What kind of** asks about the particular variety or type of something.
	(q) **What** *did* you *do* last night? **What** *is* Mary *doing*?	I studied. Reading a book.	**What** + *a form of* **do** is used to ask questions about activities.
	(r) **What countries** did you visit? **What time** did she come? **What color** is his hair?	Italy and Spain. Seven o'clock. Dark brown.	**What** may accompany a noun.
	(s) **What** *is* Ed *like*? (t) **What** *is* the weather *like*?	He's kind and friendly. Hot and humid.	**What** + **be like** asks for a general description of qualities.
	(u) **What** *does* Ed *look like*? (v) **What** *does* her house *look like*?	He's tall and has dark hair. It's a two-story,* red brick house.	**What** + **look like** asks for a physical description.
WHICH	(w) I have two pens. **Which pen** do you want? **Which one** do you want? **Which do** you want? (x) **Which book** should I buy?	The blue one. That one.	**Which** is used instead of **what** when a question concerns choosing from a definite, known quantity or group.
	(y) **Which countries** did he visit? **What countries** did he visit? (z) **Which class** are you in? **What class** are you in?	Peru and Chile. This class.	In some cases, there is little difference in meaning between **which** and **what** when they accompany a noun, as in (y) and (z).

*American English: *a two-**story** house.*
  British English: *a two-**storey** house.*

B-3 SHORTENED YES/NO QUESTIONS

(a) *Going to bed now?* = *Are you going to bed now?* (b) *Finish your work?* = *Did you finish your work?* (c) *Want to go to the movie with us?* = *Do you want to go to the movie with us?*	Sometimes in spoken English, the auxiliary and the subject *you* are dropped from a yes/no question, as in (a), (b), and (c).

B-4 NEGATIVE QUESTIONS

(a) *Doesn't she live* in the dormitory? (b) *Does she not live* in the dormitory? *(very formal)*	In a yes/no question in which the verb is negative, usually a contraction (e.g., *does* + *not* = *doesn't*) is used, as in (a). Example (b) is very formal and is usually not used in everyday speech. Negative questions are used to indicate the speaker's idea (i.e., what s/he believes is or is not true) or attitude (e.g., surprise, shock, annoyance, anger).
(c) Bob returns to his dorm room after his nine o'clock class. Matt, his roommate, is there. Bob is surprised. Bob says, *"What are you doing here? Aren't you supposed to be in class now?"*	In (c): Bob believes that Matt is supposed to be in class now. *Expected answer:* **Yes**.
(d) Alice and Mary are at home. Mary is about to leave on a trip, and Alice is going to take her to the airport. Alice says, *"It's already two o'clock. We'd better leave for the airport. Doesn't your plane leave at three?"*	In (d): Alice believes that Mary's plane leaves at three. She is asking the negative question to make sure that her information is correct. *Expected answer:* **Yes**.
(e) The teacher is talking to Jim about a test he failed. The teacher is surprised that Jim failed the test because he usually does very well. The teacher says: *"What happened? Didn't you study?"*	In (e): The teacher believes that Jim did not study. *Expected answer:* **No**.
(f) Barb and Ron are riding in a car. Ron is driving. He comes to a corner where there is a stop sign, but he does not stop the car. Barb is shocked. Barb says, *"What's the matter with you? Didn't you see that stop sign?"*	In (f): Barb believes that Ron did not see the stop sign. *Expected answer:* **No**.

B-5 TAG QUESTIONS

(a) Jack *can* come, *can't* he? (b) Fred *can't* come, *can* he?	A tag question is a question added at the end of a sentence. Speakers use tag questions chiefly to make sure their information is correct or to seek agreement.★

AFFIRMATIVE SENTENCE **+** NEGATIVE TAG → AFFIRMATIVE ANSWER EXPECTED

Mary *is* here,	*isn't* she?	Yes, she is.
You *like* tea,	*don't* you?	Yes, I do.
They *have left*,	*haven't* they?	Yes, they have.

NEGATIVE SENTENCE **+** AFFIRMATIVE TAG → NEGATIVE ANSWER EXPECTED

Mary *isn't* here,	*is* she?	No, she isn't.
You *don't like* tea,	*do* you?	No, I don't.
They *haven't left*,	*have* they?	No, they haven't.

(c) ***This/That*** is your book, isn't *it?* ***These/Those*** are yours, aren't *they?*	The tag pronoun for ***this/that*** = ***it***. The tag pronoun for ***these/those*** = ***they***.
(d) ***There is*** a meeting tonight, ***isn't there?***	In sentences with ***there + be***, ***there*** is used in the tag.
(e) ***Everything*** is okay, isn't *it?* (f) ***Everyone*** took the test, didn't *they?*	Personal pronouns are used to refer to indefinite pronouns. ***They*** is usually used in a tag to refer to ***everyone***, ***everybody***, ***someone***, ***somebody***, ***no one***, ***nobody***.
(g) ***Nothing is*** wrong, *is* it? (h) ***Nobody called*** on the phone, ***did*** they? (i) You*'ve **never been*** there, ***have*** you?	Sentences with negative words take affirmative tags.
(j) ***I am*** supposed to be here, ***am I not?*** (k) ***I am*** supposed to be here, ***aren't I?***	In (j): ***am I not?*** is formal English. In (k): ***aren't I?*** is common in spoken English.

★A tag question may be spoken:

  (1) with a rising intonation if the speaker is truly seeking to ascertain that his/her information, idea, belief is correct (e.g., *Ann lives in an apartment, doesn't she?*); OR

  (2) with a falling intonation if the speaker is expressing an idea with which s/he is almost certain the listener will agree (e.g., *It's a nice day today, isn't it?*).

UNIT C: Contractions

C CONTRACTIONS

IN SPEAKING: In everyday spoken English, certain forms of **be** and auxiliary verbs are usually contracted with pronouns, nouns, and question words.

IN WRITING: (1) In written English, contractions with pronouns are common in informal writing, but not generally acceptable in formal writing.

(2) Contractions with nouns and question words are, for the most part, rarely used in writing. A few of these contractions may be found in quoted dialogue in stories or in very informal writing, such as a chatty letter to a good friend, but most of them are rarely if ever written.

In the following, quotation marks indicate that the contraction is frequently spoken, but rarely if ever written.

	WITH PRONOUNS	**WITH NOUNS**	**WITH QUESTION WORDS**
am	*I'm* reading a book.	Ø	*"What'm"* I supposed to do?
is	*She's* studying. *It's* going to rain.	My *"book's"* on the table. *Mary's* at home.	*Where's* Sally? *Who's* that man?
are	*You're* working hard. *They're* waiting for us.	My *"books're"* on the table. The *"teachers're"* at a meeting.	*"What're"* you doing? *"Where're"* they going?
has	*She's* been here for a year. *It's* been cold lately.	My *"book's"* been stolen! *Sally's* never met him.	*Where's* Sally been living? *What's* been going on?
have	*I've* finished my work. *They've* never met you.	The *"books've"* been sold. The *"students've"* finished the test.	*"Where've"* they been? *"How've"* you been?
had	*He'd* been waiting for us. *We'd* forgotten about it.	The *"books'd"* been sold. *"Mary'd"* never met him before.	*"Where'd"* you been before that? *"Who'd"* been there before you?
did	Ø	Ø	*"What'd"* you do last night? *"How'd"* you do on the test?
will	*I'll* come later. *She'll* help us.	The *"weather'll"* be nice tomorrow. *"John'll"* be coming soon.	*"Who'll"* be at the meeting? *"Where'll"* you be at ten?
would	*He'd* like to go there. *They'd* come if they could.	My *"friends'd"* come if they could. *"Mary'd"* like to go there, too.	*"Where'd"* you like to go?

UNIT D: Negatives

D-1 USING *NOT* AND OTHER NEGATIVE WORDS

(a) AFFIRMATIVE: The earth is round. (b) NEGATIVE: The earth is **not** flat.	*Not* expresses a *negative* idea.

AUX + *NOT* + MAIN VERB (c) I **will** **not** **go** there. I **have** **not** **gone** there. I **am** **not** **going** there. I **was** **not** there. I **do** **not** **go** there. He **does** **not** **go** there. I **did** **not** **go** there.	*Not* immediately follows an auxiliary verb or *be*. (Note: If there is more than one auxiliary, **not** comes immediately after the first auxiliary: *I **will** **not** be going there.*) *Do* or *does* is used with **not** to make a simple present verb (except **be**) negative. *Did* is used with **not** to make a simple past verb (except **be**) negative.

CONTRACTIONS OF AUXILIARY VERBS WITH *NOT*

*are not = aren't**	*has not = hasn't*	*was not = wasn't*
cannot = can't	*have not = haven't*	*were not = weren't*
could not = couldn't	*had not = hadn't*	*will not = won't*
did not = didn't	*is not = isn't*	*would not = wouldn't*
does not = doesn't	*must not = mustn't*	
do not = don't	*should not = shouldn't*	

(d) I almost **never** go there. I have **hardly ever** gone there. (e) There's **no** chalk in the drawer.	In addition to **not**, the following are negative adverbs: *never, rarely, seldom* *hardly (ever), scarcely (ever), barely (ever)* *No* also expresses a negative idea.

COMPARE: *NOT* VS. *NO* (f) I **do not have** any money. (g) I have **no money**.	*Not* is used to make a verb negative, as in (f). *No* is used as an adjective in front of a noun (e.g., *money*), as in (g). Note: (f) and (g) have the same meaning.

*Sometimes in spoken English you will hear "ain't." It means "am not," "isn't," or "aren't." *Ain't* is not considered proper English, but many people use *ain't* regularly, and it is also frequently used for humor.

D-2 AVOIDING DOUBLE NEGATIVES

(a) *INCORRECT:* I *don't* have *no* money. (b) CORRECT: I *don't* have **any** money. CORRECT: I have **no** money.	(a) is an example of a "double negative," i.e., a confusing and grammatically incorrect sentence that contains two negatives in the same clause. One clause should contain only one negative.*

*NOTE: Negatives in two different clauses in the same sentence cause no problems; for example:
> A person who **doesn't** have love **can't** be truly happy.
> I **don't** know why he **isn't** here.

D-3 BEGINNING A SENTENCE WITH A NEGATIVE WORD

(a) ***Never will I do*** that again! (b) ***Rarely have I eaten*** better food. (c) ***Hardly ever does he come*** to class on time.	When a negative word begins a sentence, the subject and verb are inverted (i.e., question word order is used).*

*Beginning a sentence with a negative word is relatively uncommon in everyday usage, but is used when the speaker/writer wishes to emphasize the negative element of the sentence and be expressive.

Never will I ride a rollercoaster again!
It's just too scary!

UNIT E: Preposition Combinations

E PREPOSITION COMBINATIONS WITH ADJECTIVES AND VERBS

A
be absent from
be accused of
be accustomed to
be acquainted with
be addicted to
be afraid of
   agree with
be angry at, with
be annoyed with, by
   apologize for
   apply to, for
   approve of
   argue with, about
   arrive in, at
be associated with
be aware of

B
   believe in
   blame for
be blessed with
be bored with, by

C
be capable of
   care about, for
be cluttered with
be committed to
   compare to, with
   complain about, of
be composed of
be concerned about
be connected to
   consist of
be content with
   contribute to
be convinced of
be coordinated with
   count (up)on
be covered with
be crowded with

D
   decide (up)on
be dedicated to
   depend (up)on
be devoted to
be disappointed in, with
be discriminated against
   distinguish from
be divorced from

   be done with
   dream of, about
be dressed in

E
be engaged in, to
be envious of
be equipped with
   escape from
   excel in, at
be excited about
be exhausted from
   excuse for
be exposed to

F
be faithful to
be familiar with
   feel like
   fight for
be filled with
be finished with
be fond of
   forget about
   forgive for
be friendly to, with
be frightened of, by
be furnished with

G
be gone from
be grateful to, for
be guilty of

H
   hide from
   hope for

I
be innocent of
   insist (up)on
be interested in
   introduce to
be involved in

J
be jealous of

K
   keep from
be known for

L
be limited to
be located in
   look forward to

M
be made of, from
be married to

O
   object to
be opposed to

P
   participate in
be patient with
be pleased with
be polite to
   pray for
be prepared for
   prevent from
   prohibit from
be protected from
be proud of
   provide with

Q
be qualified for

R
   recover from
be related to
be relevant to
   rely (up)on
be remembered for
   rescue from
   respond to
be responsible for

S
be satisfied with
be scared of, by
   stare at
   stop from
   subscribe to
   substitute for
   succeed in

T
   take advantage of
   take care of
   talk about, of
be terrified of, by
   thank for
   think about, of
be tired of, from

U
be upset with
be used to

V
   vote for

W
be worried about

UNIT F: Connectives to Give Examples and to Continue an Idea

F-1 CONNECTIVES TO GIVE EXAMPLES

(a) There are many interesting places to visit in the city. *For example*, the botanical garden has numerous displays of plants from all over the world. (b) There are many interesting places to visit in the city. The art museum, *for instance*, has an excellent collection of modern paintings.	*For example* and *for instance* have the same meaning. They are often used as transitions. (See Chart 19-3, p. 96.)
(c) There are many interesting places to visit in the city, *e.g.*, the botanical garden and the art museum. (d) There are many interesting places to visit in the city, *for example*, the botanical garden or the art museum.	*e.g.* = *for example* (*e.g.* is an abbreviation of the Latin phrase *exempli gratia*.)* (c) and (d) have the same meaning.
(e) I prefer to wear casual clothes, *such as* jeans and a sweatshirt. (f) Some countries, *such as* Brazil and Canada, are big. (g) Countries *such as* Brazil and Canada are big. (h) *Such* countries *as* Brazil and Canada are big.	*such as* = *for example* (f), (g), and (h) have essentially the same meaning even though the pattern varies.**

*Punctuation note: Periods are used with *e.g.* in American English. Periods are generally not used with *eg* in British English.

**Punctuation note:
- (1) When the "*such as* phrase" can be omitted without substantially changing the meaning of the sentence, commas are used.
  Example: Some words, such as *know* and *see*, are verbs. *(Commas are used.)*
- (2) No commas are used when the "*such as* phrase" gives essential information about the noun to which it refers.
  Example: Words such as *know* and *see* are verbs. *(No commas are used.)*

F-2 CONNECTIVES TO CONTINUE THE SAME IDEA

(a) The city provides many cultural opportunities. It has an excellent art museum. *Moreover,* *Furthermore,* } it has a fine symphony orchestra. *In addition,*	*Moreover*, *furthermore*, and *in addition* mean "also." They are *transitions*. (See Chart 19-3, p. 96.)
(b) The city provides many cultural opportunities. *In addition to* } an excellent art museum, it has *Besides* a fine symphony orchestra.	In (b): *In addition to* and *besides** are used as prepositions. They are followed by an object *(museum)*, not a clause.

*COMPARE: *Besides* means "in addition to."
   Beside means "next to"; e.g., *I sat beside my friend.*

INDEX

Able to, 53, 55 *(Look on pages 53 and 55.)*	The numbers following the words listed in the index refer to page numbers in the main text.
Be, A4 *(Look in the back part of this book on the fourth page of the Appendix.)*	The index numbers preceded by the letter "A" (e.g., A4) refer to pages in the Appendix, which is found in the last part of the text. The main text ends on page 104, and the appendix immediately follows. Page 104 is followed by page A1.
Continuous tenses, 2*fn.* *(Look at the footnote on page 2.)*	Information given in the footnotes to charts and exercises is noted by the page number plus the abbreviation *fn.*